IMAGES
of America

SPARTANBURG COUNTY
IN WORLD WAR II

In honor of Spartanburg County veterans, their families, and those who
served tirelessly on the homefront.
In memory of those who sacrificed their lives.

BACKGROUND

More than 6,000 people from Spartanburg County served with distinction during World War II. Although their roles varied, there was a shared desire that each return home. Naomi S. (Mrs. H.T.) Littlejohn of Spartanburg was the mother of four sons serving concurrently during World War II. As did mothers everywhere, Mrs. Littlejohn, praying fervently for her beloved sons, assured them that she, in essence, "hung a prayer on every star for each of them."

In addition to hanging prayers on stars, Spartanburg County families hung Blue Stars in their windows for family members in service. Blue Stars became Gold Stars with the death of a loved one. Sadly, one of Naomi S. Littlejohn's four sons—Jesse Broadus, one of the twins—did not return. As Naomi's poem states, he would always live in her heart.

No Gold Star

There'll be no Gold Star in my window
For the dear lad who went away
On a bright summer morning
With a heart so light and gay.

He answered the call of duty
Giving his life at the very last
That men might live in peace
And freedom and that fear be past.

Of course I'll grieve for him
Keep a place for him set apart,
But no Gold Star goes in my window,
For he'll always live in my heart.

—Naomi S. Littlejohn
(The photo of Naomi S. [Mrs. H.T.] Littlejohn is courtesy of William B. Littlejohn.)

(*on the cover*) The cover photo is courtesy of Technical Sergeant John B. Reash (back row, fifth from left) 323rd Bomb Squadron, 91st Bomb Group, Eighth Air Force. Reash was flight engineer and top turret gunner on the "Nine O Nine," a B-17G. He flew 35 missions—not the 25 required.

IMAGES
of America

SPARTANBURG COUNTY
IN WORLD WAR II

Anita Price Davis and James M. Walker

ARCADIA
PUBLISHING

Published by Arcadia Publishing
Charleston SC, Chicago IL, Portsmouth NH, San Francisco CA

Printed in the United States of America

Library of Congress Catalog Card Number: 2004109622

For all general information contact Arcadia Publishing at:
Telephone 843-853-2070
Fax 843-853-0044
E-mail sales@arcadiapublishing.com
For customer service and orders:
Toll-Free 1-888-313-2665

Visit us on the Internet at www.arcadiapublishing.com

FOREWORD

Real Heroes: Rutherford County Men Who Made the Supreme Sacrifice in World War II (Anita Price Davis with James M. Walker) was the first book in a series telling of the sacrifices and services of local veterans and their families. *Real Heroes* began the series by honoring each of the 140+ Rutherford County, North Carolina, men who lost their lives during World War II; among these heroes was Arthur F. Price, the father of Anita Price Davis.

Soon after the publication of *Real Heroes*, local residents began to ask: "What about us who came home? Where is our book?" or "What about those of us who served on the homefront? May we have our stories told?" *Images of America: Rutherford County in World War II* (Anita Price Davis and James M. Walker) began preserving their important accounts. After its publication, phone calls and inquiries poured in from others not in either previous volume. The series continued with *Images of America: Rutherford County in World War II, Volume II*.

Because Anita worked in Spartanburg County, South Carolina, and because she knew and respected the county residents, she and Jim wanted to record their stories. They have many people to thank. Converse College endorsed Anita's beginning yet another project; Converse students helped with the primary research. Fernwood Baptist Church hosted the veterans in its peaceful, accessible facilities; more than 100 people arrived. Fernwood member Louise Hunt expertly scanned the materials. Helen Collins provided access to many materials. Tom C. Moore, the pastor of Green Street Baptist Church, personally delivered information for his parishioners. The Converse Communications Office, the *Herald-Journal*, Bill Drake at WSPA (Pottery Road), Pic-A-Book, and others helped and encouraged. Roger Wesley Goodwin and his daughter Meg Goodwin Cooksey generously shared their photo albums.

The result of these united efforts is *Images of America: Spartanburg County in World War II*. To include all the veterans we had contacted, we had to reduce the sizes of their images and stories to meet the publisher's format. Although we regret that we could not give each person several pages, we have at least begun. We are grateful to the vets for their sacrifices and for their friendship.

CONTENTS

In his poem "Just Remember," M.Sgt. Walter C. Garrett reminded us all where our loyalties should be.

Just Remember

When your life seems hard and dreary
And your burdens are hard to bear,
Just think of the boys who are fighting
Dig in and do your share.

When you wake up in the morning
And you dread the day ahead,
Just remember when night comes
Then you go to bed.

So when you feel like quitting
Or you think you need more pay,
Just remember the boys who are fighting.
They are called and have to stay.

So when you are asked to buy War Bonds
Or give the Red Cross a hand,
Remember it's all for freedom,
No dictator will rule this land.

M.Sgt. Walter C. Garrett (1944)

Ten years later, while he was still in the service, Walter C. Garrett married Margaret L. Hughes on February 13, 1954. This is a photo of the newlyweds. (Courtesy of Walter C. Garrett.)

INTRODUCTION

In the late 1930s, Europe was falling under the influence of Nazism, Fascism, and Communism. The Japanese Empire, characterized by its totalitarian form of government, was striving for hegemony (domination) over East Asia. Ripples of this turmoil were spreading throughout the world.

In the pre-war years, German Chancellor Adolf Hitler gives the Nazi salute as he inspects the crew of the battleship *Schleswig-Holstein*. Hitler was rapidly re-arming the German military as he planned his world conquest. (Courtesy of the collection of H.P. Harrill.)

The 1930s would bring hardship to American lives and would focus our attention on internal matters to the exclusion of foreign affairs. These students of Whitney School would endure and overcome the trials of the era; their hardships would strengthen them for the decade that was to come. Many of these locals would answer the call to serve. Some, like Volney Lee Byars (fifth from left, back row) would pay the ultimate price. (Courtesy of Billy Joe Byars.)

The photo of the Spartanburg High School band in 1941 shows Paul Skelton (far right, third row) and David Bishop (second from right, third row). Soon they, like others in the band, would trade their trombones for implements of war. Both of these young men would eventually become POWs. (Courtesy of Paul Skelton.)

One

War Comes to Spartanburg County (December 7, 1941)
Pearl Harbor

On December 7, 1941, 353 Japanese naval aircraft from 6 carriers suddenly attacked the American fleet at Pearl Harbor, Hawaiian Islands, and the nearby navy and army bases. Servicemen and civilians alike were staggered and stunned by the surprise assault, which came without a formal declaration of war.

Spartanburg County suffered its first fatalities when the USS *Arizona* sank and the USS *Oklahoma* capsized. Carpenter's Mate 3rd Class Wayne Alman Lewis of Arcadia and Seaman 1st Class Vernon Russell White of Spartanburg died as a result of the Japanese bombs. Also killed was Harold C. Davis's cousin, Fire Controlman 1st Class Hubert Paul Clement of the *Oklahoma*. Gunner's Mate 3rd Class John Warton Rampley of Spartanburg was a survivor of the attack on the USS *Arizona*. In a *Honolulu Star Bulletin* article on December 6, 2001, Rampley recalled "leaping to his battle station," "lots of explosions," "being unable to see anything," "rivets popping out of the metal," and "bolts flying through the air." (Courtesy of U.S. Navy.)

Sgt. Jay B. Strange, Service Company, 35th Infantry, enlisted in August 1939. On December 7, 1941, he had spent—he thought—his last night in Honolulu and had just finished breakfast in town. "They caught us with our pants down," he said later. In a frantic cab ride to Schofield Barracks, Japanese planes strafed the highway; Strange's cab lost a mirror and a left tire. He and six other servicemen lifted the vehicle to change the tire; they did not use a jack. For his services in Pearl Harbor, Guadalcanal, northern Solomons Island, and the Philippine Islands, Sergeant Strange earned the Asiatic-Pacific Campaign Medal with four Bronze Service Stars, American Defense Medal with Bronze Service Star, the Philippine Liberation Medal, the Combat Infantryman's Badge, and the Good Conduct Medal. (Courtesy of Jay B. Strange.)

Even in his later years, Harold C. Davis (December 13, 1919–May 20, 2004) remembered well the attack at Pearl Harbor. CWO Harold Davis came on deck when he heard the explosions because he thought it was a practice exercise, but when he saw the Rising Suns on the planes, he knew it was for real. Later in the war, he served aboard the USS *Birmingham*. A patriot to the end of his life, Davis said from his bed on May 12, 2004, that he would be willing to serve his country again if called. (Courtesy of Mrs. Nena [Harold C.] Davis.)

Two

IMPEDING THE JAPANESE (1942–1943)

SOUTHWEST PACIFIC, SOLOMON ISLANDS, NEW GUINEA

As 1942 began, the Imperial Japanese Fleet ranged with amazing swiftness over vast areas of the Western Pacific and Eastern Indian Oceans. In six short months, the Japanese Imperial Forces subjugated Wake Island, Hong Kong, Singapore, the Netherlands East Indies, Thailand, Burma, the Philippines, and Northern New Guinea. For half a year, the forces of Emperor Hirohito had run wild without impediment until the Japanese commanders became intoxicated with "victory disease," a feeling of invincibility and inevitability.

The Pacific Fleet of the U.S. Navy under the command of Adm. Chester Nimitz and U.S. Army forces in the Southwest Pacific under the command of Gen. Douglas MacArthur finally blocked further advances in the Coral Sea, at Midway Island, at Guadalcanal, and in Southern New Guinea.

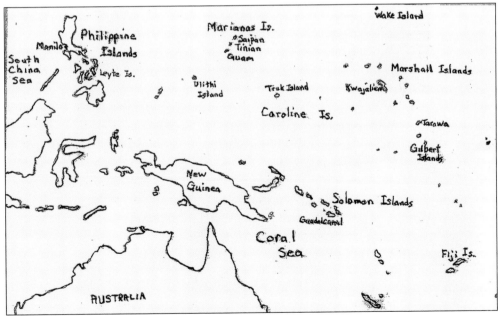

The sketch map is courtesy of James M. Walker.

The USS *Lexington* sank while helping stop the Japanese drive on Port Moresby, New Guinea, in May 1942. Despite the loss of *Lady Lex*, the American victory prevented further Japanese advances in the Coral Sea. In June 1942, the Japanese Adm. Isokoru Yamamoto with the Combined Fleet progressed across the Central Pacific to attack Midway Island. The resulting American victory threw the Japanese on the defensive. (Courtesy of U.S. Navy.)

On August 7, 1942, the 1st Marine Division came ashore on Guadalcanal in the Solomon Islands, which saw some of the bitterest fighting in the entire Pacific War. The U.S. Army later reinforced the Marines and forced the Japanese to evacuate the island in February 1943. (Courtesy of U.S. Army.)

Three

THE AIR WAR (1942–1945)
EUROPE AND THE PACIFIC

In July 1942, the U.S. Army Air Force began a strategic bombing campaign over occupied Europe. These raids from bases in England sought to destroy the war-making capabilities of the Axis adversary. By devastating and demolishing railways, factories, and troop concentrations and by interdicting communication, troop movements, and supply routes, the Allied Forces continued their relentless bombardment of its foe. The 8th Air Force, in cooperation with the Bomber Command of the British Royal Air Force, executed around-the-clock operations against the enemy. The 15th Air Force from bases in North Africa and, later, Italy joined in the bombardment of the southern and eastern portion of the German Reich.

T.Sgt. John B. Reash (left) and a fellow air crewman prepare equipment for a mission over Germany. These two men are representatives of the thousands of U.S. Army Air Force personnel who crewed the B-17s, B-24s, and other aircraft that brought the air war home to Hitler. (Courtesy of John B. Reash.)

Lt. Vernon M. Stokely was supply officer with the 13th Photo Recon Squadron, 7th Photo Group, 8th Air Force. Stokely's bases were Station 234 and Station 465, Oxfordshire, England. His unit, which served as "the eyes" of the 8th Air Force, flew modified P-38 *Lightnings* equipped with high-resolution cameras. During the course of the war, the group flew 5,693 operational sorties and suffered 43 pilots killed and 31 POW/MIA. The 7th Photo Recon Group received a Presidential Unit Citation for its excellence and valor. Captain Stokely earned the European-African-Middle Eastern (EAME) Campaign Medal with six Bronze Service Stars, a World War II Victory Medal, and the Good Conduct Medal. (Courtesy of Vernon M. Stokely.)

Lt. Arthur Hammond was the navigator on the B-17G "Capt'n and His 'Kids,'" which took its name from characters in the comic strip *The Katzenjammer Kids* by Rudolph Dirks. (Courtesy of Arthur Hammond and family.)

14

Arthur Hammond retired as colonel from the U.S. Air Force on September 19, 1963, and as commander of the 9314th Air Force Recovery Squadron, Spartanburg, South Carolina. Hammond holds the Distinguished Flying Cross, Air Medal with Three Oak Leaf Clusters, and EAME Campaign Medal. The Spartanburg community knows him well also through his business interest: HBJ Home Furnishings. (Courtesy of Arthur Hammond and family.)

T.Sgt. John B. Reash, 323rd Bomb Squadron, 91st Bomb Group, 8th Air Force, flew 35 missions over occupied Europe. Reash was flight engineer and top turret gunner on the "Nine O Nine." Here Reash stands before the B-17G that flew 140 missions. Sgt. Reash suffered wounds from flak fragments and received the Purple Heart, Distinguished Flying Cross, Air Medal, EAME Campaign Medal with two Bronze Service Stars, and Good Conduct Medal. (Courtesy of John B. Reash.)

15

Maj. William Earle Hendrix Jr., 784th Bomb Squadron, 466th Bomb Group, 8th Air Force, piloted the B-24J *Liberator* on 24 missions. His base was Attlebridge near Norwich, England. Major Hendrix (third from left, back row) received the Distinguished Flying Cross, Air Medal, EAME Campaign Medal, Good Conduct Medal, and others. Hendrix participated as a pilot of a C-54 (a cargo plane) during the Berlin Air Lift of December 1948. Here he and his crew pose before their plane, the "Black Cat," for his missions over Germany. (Courtesy of William E. Hendrix Jr. and Richard W. Hendrix.)

While the "heavies" of the 8th Air Force pounded the German cities, smaller aircraft like the B-26 and A-26 conducted tactical air strikes in support of U.S. ground forces. Lt. James Edward Lockery served as assistant engineer of a unit in England that helped maintain and service the B-26 *Marauders*. After his transfer to France, Lockery continued the same duty with the newer, more sophisticated A-26 *Invader* bombers. (Courtesy of James Edward Lockery.)

The Axis fiercely contested the Allied bombing missions that originated in England. In the air, Luftwaffe fighters sought to annihilate the attackers. On the ground near the main targets, massive anti-aircraft batteries attempted to blast from the skies the bombers approaching their objectives. (Courtesy of U.S. Air Force.)

S.Sgt. Jacob "Jake" T. DeLamar was a tail gunner of a B-17 *Flying Fortress* of the 418th Bomb Squadron, 100th Bomb Group, 8th Air Force. During his 14th mission, over Frankfurt, Germany, on February 4, 1944, DeLamar's plane lost an engine to German fire. When the second engine failed, the plane made a successful emergency landing in a cornfield. After his capture, DeLamar suffered in a POW stalag in Lithuania and endured a 300-mile forced march back to Germany. DeLamar endured frozen feet and several bouts of bronchitis and pneumonia before his liberation. He recalled receiving a food package of Spam, corned beef, and milk with the fat removed. (Courtesy of Clara F. DeLamar.)

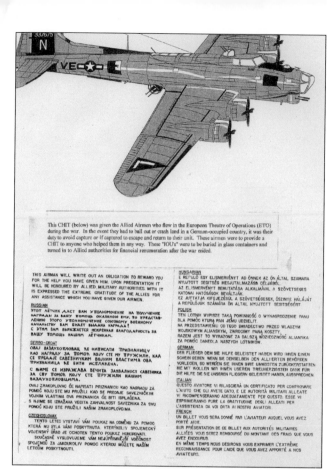

This CHIT (below) was given the Allied Airmen who flew in the European Theatre of Operations (ETO) during the war. In the event they had to bail out or crash land in a German-occupied country, it was their duty to avoid capture or if captured to escape and return to their unit. These airmen were to provide a CHIT to anyone who helped them in any way. These "IOU's" were to be buried in glass containers and turned in to Allied authorities for financial renumeration after the war ended.

While the air crews of the 8th Air Force received the press, another U.S. Army Air Force was also relentlessly pounding the foe. From bases in Libya and later in Italy, aircraft of the 15th Air Force bombed a variety of targets in the Balkans, Austria, Hungary, eastern Germany, Poland, and northern Italy. The objectives included oil refineries, marshalling yards, ordnance depots, supply depots, ammo dumps, and sundry other facilities. T.Sgt. Joe K. Kelley, 414th Bomb Squadron, 97th Bomb Group, 15th Air Force, was a radio operator machine gunner on a B-17. Joe recalls the "chit" that airmen forced to land might present to residents helping them in occupied countries; at the end of the war the federal government made good on the promises for aiding its service personnel. (Courtesy of Joe K. Kelley.)

When Joe K. Kelley had his portrait made during his time in Italy, he had grown a beard. When his mom saw the photo, she said, "Buy War Bonds! Send this poor boy home!" These prayers were answered when he returned home safely. Kelley received for his services the EAME Campaign Medal with four Bronze Service Stars, the Air Medal with Three Oak Leaf Clusters, and the Good Conduct Medal. (Courtesy of Joe K. Kelley.)

Second Lt. David L. Bishop Jr. (fourth from left, first row) was with the 324th Bomb Squadron, 91st Bomb Group, 8th Air Force, based at Bassingbourn, England. On his third mission as a co-pilot on November 26, 1944, his plane was shot down by flak and some German fighter planes near Hannover, Germany. After capture and interrogation, he and 23 other "roommates" received internment in Stalag Luft I near Barth, Germany. There were about 9,000 POWs in the camp. (Courtesy of David L. Bishop Jr.)

This cartoon, given to Bishop by a "roomie," illustrates how the POWs maintained their morale under very trying conditions. After an approximate seven-month imprisonment, Bishop and his fellow POWs received liberation by the Soviet Red Army and repatriation to the Allies after approximately two weeks. (Courtesy of David L. Bishop Jr.)

Thomas Wilton Bonner received a commission in the U.S. Army as a second lieutenant upon his completion of R.O.T.C. training at Wofford College. Recalled to active duty in the U.S. Army Air Corps, he served for four years. He received a letter of commendation from Gen. H.H. "Hap" Arnold, commander in chief of the U.S. Army Air Forces. After the war, Bonner served as principal at Chesnee Elementary School, Chesnee, South Carolina. (Courtesy of Alice B. Greene.)

In the first few months of the Pacific War, the main effort of the U.S. Army Air Forces was to support U.S. Marine Corps and Army units in the recapture of Japanese-held territories. Using a wide variety of aircraft and operating from diverse bases from India to New Guinea to the islands of the Central Pacific, Americans persevered in their goals in the Pacific Theater. (Courtesy of U.S. Air Forces.)

S.Sgt. Fred Alvin Clayton was top turret gunner on a B-25; he participated in operations over New Guinea with the 345th Bomb Group, "Tree Top Terrors," 5th Air Force. (Courtesy of Gladys Clayton Mills.)

S.Sgt. Fred Alvin Clayton (right) died in action on May 21, 1944, when his B-25 was shot down on the north coast of New Guinea near Wewak. (Courtesy of Gladys Clayton Mills.)

S.Sgt. Fred Alvin Clayton's brother S.Sgt. Clifford Thomas Clayton, Headquarters Battery, 251st Field Artillery Battalion, arrived in New Guinea. Sadly, however, neither knew that the other had a station there. They had no reunion before the death of Fred Alvin. Clifford Thomas received the Purple Heart, the Good Conduct Medal, the American Defense Service Medal with one Service Star, the Asiatic Pacific Campaign Medal, the Philippine Liberation Ribbon, the World War II Army of Occupation (Japan), the World War II Victory Medal, and the Honorable Discharge Medal. (Courtesy of Gladys Clayton Mills.)

First Lt. Henry P. Elias of the 23rd Fighter Group, 14th Air Force, died in action while serving in China. For his services, Elias received two Silver Stars and a posthumous Purple Heart. "Chink" was 23 years of age at his death. (Courtesy of Fred A. Elias.)

Pictured here are, from left to right, (front row) S.Sgt. Victor Elias, Henry's brother and a top turret gunner on a B-24; and Fred A. Elias; (back row) father Alexander E. Elias; brother George Elias with the U.S. Army Air Forces; and brother James F. Elias, father of five children and not in the service. (Courtesy of Fred A. Elias.)

Aviation Machinist's Mate 2nd Class Nathan "Gremlin" Hodge, VB-104, was the bow gunner of Crew 13 on "the Vulnerable Virgin," a B-24 bomber. AMM2C Nathan Hodge stands far left. (Courtesy of Nathan Hodge and David Hodge.)

From its base in the Russell Islands, the VB-104 conducted operations over Rabaul, Kavieng, Bougainville, and other islands in the Southwest Pacific. Hodge and crew were testing some new equipment on "Donald's Duck" when they crash landed, killing one crew member and injuring Hodge (the bow gunner) by catapulting him from the nose position and hurling him 150 feet down the runway. Hodge received a steel plate in his nose after arriving in the United States for treatment. Hodge continued his career in the U.S. Navy until 1960; when asked about the crew's medals, he commented, "We didn't get a damn thing." (Courtesy of Nathan Hodge and David Hodge.)

During 1944, 2nd Lt. Dan Ray Arrowood piloted a B-24 with the 400th Squadron, 90th Bomb Group, 5th Air Force, from Biak, New Guinea. This photo shows him in full flight gear during his stateside training. (Courtesy of Dan Ray Arrowood.)

Throughout 1945, 2nd Lt. Dan Ray Arrowood served as a pilot of a C-46 in the 7th Squadron, 2nd Combat Cargo Group, 54th Troop Carrier Wing, 5th Air Force. Here he is in the cockpit of his aircraft. The 2nd Cargo Group supported Allied operations in the Western Pacific and occupied Japan. Arrowood received the Asiatic-Pacific Campaign Medal with three Bronze Service Stars, the American Theater Campaign Medal, and the World War II Victory Medal. He married Mary Wilson Tucker Arrowood. (Courtesy of Dan Ray Arrowood.)

Establishing a series of air bases in Asia and the Pacific Islands was a requirement for the strategic bombing campaign. Using the long-range B-24 and the newly introduced B-29 *Superfortress*, Americans demonstrated their power over the forces of the Emperor Hirohito. This B-24 *Liberator* of the 864th Bombardment Squadron, 494th Bomb Group (H), 7th Air Force had as its pilot 1st Lt. Alfred O. Schmitz (far right, back row). (Courtesy of Alfred O. Schmitz.)

Lt. Alfred O. Schmitz participated in the air offense against the Eastern Mandates, the Western Pacific, Southern Philippines, Luzon, the Ryukyus, China, and Japan. Schmitz received the American Campaign Medal, the Asiatic Pacific Campaign Medal, the Good Conduct Medal, and the World War II Victory Medal. After the war, Dr. Alfred O. Schmitz served from 1961 until 1989 as a professor of philosophy at Converse College. (Courtesy of Alfred O. Schmitz.)

The newly introduced B-29 *Superfortress* bombed the Japanese home islands from bases in Southern China. Air bases in India transported personnel, spare parts, ordnance, fuel, and supplies to maintain maximum efficiency of the 14th Air Force. The planes that flew these missions over "the hump" from India to China were C-54s of the 2nd Ferrying Group Division, Air Transport Command. Sgt. Linwood Hackett recalls, "The aircraft were magnificent by any measure." During his time in service, he flew 2,500 hours as a crewmember. (Courtesy of Linwood Hackett.)

Ernest "Ernie" Alford Billings trained as a P-47 pilot; his next assignment would have taken him to Japan, but the war ended. Billings retired as a major after 22 and a half years in the air force. Before the war, Billings was assistant manager of McClellan's Five and Ten Cents Store in downtown Spartanburg. (Courtesy of E.A. Billings.)

First Lt. Charles A. Graves, who served as a navigator on a B-29 assigned to the 330th Bomb Group, 20th Air Force, was responsible for navigating his plane "the Motley Crew" for missions of 3,000 miles. He said he would never forget the sound of the exploding anti-aircraft shells, the attack of the aircraft of the Emperor's Guard, and what Tokyo looked like the night the 20th Air Force burned it. Members of the crew received the Distinguished Flying Cross. Here Lt. Bob Hall (first on left) watches as Graves (second from left) shakes the hand of Squadron Commander Ryder. (Courtesy of Charles A. Graves.)

In his autobiography, 1st Lt. Charles A. Graves (second from left, back row) paid tribute to his mentor, Latta School Superintendent B.F. Carmichael, "the Man." Graves called Carmichael "the motivation" that helped Graves become the first honor graduate of The Citadel. Graves has pastored or co-pastored Duncan Memorial Methodist Church (the oldest Methodist church in South Carolina), Trinity Methodist Church in Spartanburg, and the Reidville Road United Methodist Church. He is pastor emeritus of Bethel United Methodist Church. (Courtesy of Charles A. Graves.)

A Marianas-based B-29 *Superfortress* is pictured flying over the Nakajima Aircraft Factory near Tokyo in 1945. (Courtesy of Charles A. Graves.)

Four

FIGHTING BACK (1942–1945)
NORTH AFRICA, SICILY, AND ITALY

President Franklin Delano Roosevelt and British Prime Minister Winston Spencer Churchill believed that an invasion of North Africa should be a first step toward an invasion of Europe. This action would be the first opportunity for the young American Army to face the veteran German troops in combat. On November 8, 1942, the Allies' amphibious attacks (Operation TORCH) hit three beaches: the Atlantic coast of French Morocco and the Mediterranean coasts of Oran and Algiers in Algeria. Upon the liberation of North Africa, the Allies moved on to invade Sicily and southern Italy in 1943, and, as a result, the Fascist regime of Benito Mussolini collapsed. The Germans bitterly contested the Allied advance, and the final surrender did not occur until May 1945.

On that fateful November day, the U.S. Army troops, under the command of Maj. Gen. George S. Patton, waded ashore and liberated Morocco in three days. (Courtesy of the U.S. Army.)

Serving as an officer in the 1st Armored Division, "Old Ironsides," which came ashore in French Morocco, was B.B. Willingham. The troops were uncertain as to what awaited them on shore. As Willingham (who retired as a major) and the other Americans stormed ashore, they met the fire of French forces still loyal to the Vichy government. (Courtesy of Mrs. B.B. Willingham and Rev. Thomas C. Moore.)

John P. Hughes graduated from The Citadel on Saturday, June 2, 1942, was commissioned as a second lieutenant, and reported for duty in the 90th Coastal Artillery Battalion on Monday, June 4, 1942. His unit was equipped with 90 mm anti-aircraft artillery and .50-caliber machine guns mounted on halftracks. They saw action in Casablanca, invaded Southern France and Lorraine, and ended the war in Munich, Germany. This image shows him outside his temporary quarters in Casablanca, French Morocco. He would later marry Jane Klim. (Courtesy of John P. Hughes.)

John P. Hughes retired as a colonel after 32 years in the U.S. Army and Reserves. This photo from the North African Campaign shows the remains of a German Ju-88 bomber. (Courtesy of John P. Hughes.)

S.Sgt. Joseph George Nohra of Company A, 38th Infantry Battalion, served as a mess sergeant in Algeria. Pictured is Joe (fourth from left), a lieutenant, and Italian POWs dressed in white and serving as waiters. Unit clubs like this helped maintain the morale of Americans abroad. (Courtesy of Joseph George Nohra.)

S. Sgt. Joseph George Nohra also served as a mess sergeant in Caserta, Italy, in one of the six palaces belonging to Victor Emmanuel III, the King of Italy (1900–1946). For his services, Joe Nohra received the EAME Campaign Medal and the Good Conduct Medal. (Courtesy of Joseph George Nohra.)

Sgt. William Loran Waldrep, Company A, 20th Engineer Combat Battalion, served at Casablanca as a stevedore, loading and unloading supplies and equipment. In 1943, while in action in Tunisia, Waldrep and his unit engaged in bridge-building, road construction, and minefield-clearing. Waldrep participated also in the invasion of Sicily. After his Sicilian service, Waldrep and other men formed a cadre for the 1277th Engineer Combat Battalion, which was preparing for the coming invasion of France. (Courtesy of William Loran Waldrep.)

Serving with Loran Waldrep (right) in
the 20th Engineer Combat Battalion was
Sgt. Frank Herbert Holland (left) from
Cary, North Carolina. Holland's three-day
pass with his buddy Waldrep resulted in
Holland's meeting Waldrep's sister Mildred
and, eventually, their marriage on August
6, 1945. The two men served together in
Casablanca, where Waldrep was honored
to serve as CQ during the Casablanca
Conference, attended by President
Roosevelt and British Prime Minister
Churchill, on December 15, 1942. Waldrep's
station was answering phones at the hotel
desk. Holland pulled outside security.
(Courtesy of Mrs. Frank Herbert [Mildred]
Holland and William Loran Waldrep.)

Frank Holland and Mildred Waldrep
Holland were on their honeymoon in Florida
when Loran arrived in Spartanburg, South
Carolina, at the end of the war. Frank
(right) and Mildred cut their honeymoon
short so that Mildred could see her brother
as soon as possible. (Courtesy of Mrs.
Frank [Mildred Waldrep] Holland.)

Clement Ralph Howell was serving with Company F, 168th Infantry, 34th Division, "Red Bull," when the Germans captured him on February 13, 1943, in North Africa. Howell and his fellow soldiers ran out to greet a tank with the American star only to find that that Germans were inside. He endured 26 months of captivity in Stalag IIIB in Fuerstenberg, Germany. (Courtesy of Mrs. Ben F. [Beth] Smart Jr.)

Pvt. 1st Class Johnny S. Green of the 15th Regiment, 3rd Division, participated in the invasion of Italy at Salerno. Wounded, he recuperated in the 118th Naval Hospital in Naples. Green returned to active duty and was captured February 1, 1944, at the Anzio Beachhead. For the next 15 and a half months, he was a German POW. His camp was in East Prussia, where the men lived off potato parings, bread, and periodic Red Cross parcels. By February 1945, the Soviet Red Army began to close in on the POW camps. "From February 20 to May 3, we walked approximately 950 miles." The 7th Armored Division liberated him outside Lubeck, Germany. (Courtesy of Johnny S. Green.)

Corporal Walter Greene (left), USMC, was the youngest of five brothers–Johnny Greene, Lee Greene, Paul Greene (U.S. Army) and Yonnie Greene (right, of the Naval Hospital, San Diego, California)–who served during World War II. Born April 9, 1926, he enlisted on March 8, 1944. After training at Parris Island, SC, and Camp Lejune, NC, he was stationed at Camp Maui, Hawaii, prior to deployment to Iwo Jima with Campany G, 2nd Battalion, 24th Marines, 4th Marine Division. After fierce cambat, he was wounded and received the Purple Heart. His unit earned the Presidential Unit Citation and the Navy Unit Commendation; Corporal Greene holds also the Asiatic Pacific Theatre Ribbon, the Good Conduct Medal, and the Honorable Discharge. He married Carol Louise Powell on November 15, 1945, and they have two girls and two boys; a daughter died in 1995. (Courtesy of Walter Greene.)

Pvt. 1st Class James W. Rankin Jr. of Company E, 15th Infantry Regiment, 3rd Division, participated in the Italian Campaign. After Rankin was injured in the left arm by shrapnel on March 23, 1944, at the Anzio Beachhead, he stated that the wound was large enough to put two fingers into. Rankin did not even realize that he was hurt until "my arm went cold." For his services, Rankin, shown here in Naples, earned the Purple Heart, Combat Infantryman's Badge, EAME Campaign Medal with two Bronze Service Stars, American Theater Campaign Medal, World War II Victory Medal, and Good Conduct Medal. (Courtesy of James W. Rankin Jr.)

One of the most ferocious battles of the Italian Campaign was at Monte Cassino. The seizure of the sixth-century Benedictine Abbey in 1944 was a joint operation that employed American, New Zealand, British, and Polish troops. Serving with the free Polish troops was Pvt. Joanna Kowalczyk, who now resides in Spartanburg County. She joined the Polish Women's Auxiliary Service on June 12, 1942, and received her discharge in September 1944. For her services, she received the British Defense Medal and the War Medal 1939–1945. (Courtesy of Joanna Kowalczyk.)

Pvt. 1st Class Guy W. Cantrell, Battery D, 435th Anti-Aircraft Artillery Battalion, served as a truck driver in his unit. The Germans captured Cantrell in Northern Italy in late 1944. He recalls arriving in Munich, Germany, on Christmas Day in 1944. He and other POWs had to work repairing the railroad tracks and buildings bombed by the Americans. After liberation, Cantrell contracted the mumps and had to convalesce for 30 days in La Havre, France. Cantrell earned the Purple Heart, American Theater Service Ribbon, EAME Campaign Medal with two Bronze Service Stars, World War II Victory Medal, and Good Conduct Medal. The former POW married Myrtle Lee McClure after two years of service. They have 4 children, 4 grandchildren, and 6 great grandchildren. (Courtesy of Guy W. Cantrell.)

This photo shows Lt. Gen. Mark W. Clark, commander of the U.S. 5th Army, attending Christmas midnight mass in Italy. Those attending the service at a tiny cathedral near Naples are (from left to right) Lt. Col. Art Sutherland, Lt. Gen. Mark W. Clark, and Maj. Gen. Alfred Gruenther, who served as Clark's chief of staff. On June 4, 1944, Clark's army would liberate Rome. (Courtesy of Alice Inez Cummins and the Office of the Chaplain, 2nd Army, Baltimore, Maryland.)

In December 1941, Robert T. Coleman Jr. was a student at the University of Texas. Rejected for military duty because of a childhood eye injury, the Texas native was determined to serve. Coleman finally received acceptance in the American Field Services, a volunteer group that served with the British Armed Forces. (Courtesy of Robert T. Coleman Jr.)

CM 86 Robert T. Coleman Jr. volunteered as an ambulance driver upon his arrival in Italy in June 1944. Later, he was one of the first Allied Service personnel to enter Florence. Upon completion of service in Italy, Coleman volunteered for service in India in August 1945. This photo shows British Field Marshal Harold R.L.G. Alexander, Supreme Allied Commander, Mediterranean, presenting the Union Jack to Maj. William Haggin Perry, AFS, in June 1945. Looking on is CM 86 Robert T. Coleman Jr. (third from left). (Courtesy of Robert T. Coleman Jr.)

Robert T. Coleman Jr. served Converse College from 1959 until 1989. In 1961, he began his tenure as president of Converse College and served in that capacity until his 1989 retirement. (Courtesy of Converse College and Dr. James G. Harrison, Mickel Archives.)

Five

THE WAR CONTINUES (1943–1944)

CBI, CLEARING THE ISLAND BARRIERS, MACARTHUR'S RETURN

By 1943, the Allies had stopped the Japanese forces and were beginning to roll them back from their conquests. The U.S. Navy and the U.S. Marine Corps were advancing across the Central Pacific. The U.S. Army, along with the Australian and New Zealand Forces, advanced upon the Philippines from the southwest. Adm. Chester Nimitz, commander in chief of the Pacific Fleet, and Gen. Douglas MacArthur, commander of the Southwest Pacific Area, directed the two-pronged offensive.

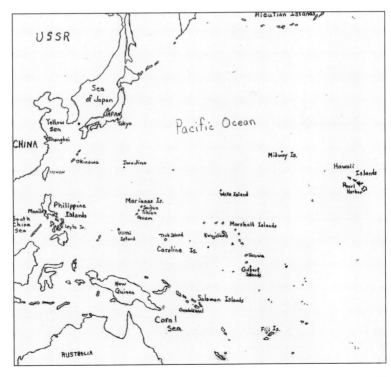

The sketch map to the right is courtesy of James M. Walker.

39

Charles W. Corne, along with some of his fellow workers from the Lyman Mills, joined the National Guard in October 1939. While on maneuvers in Florida, Charlie and his Lyman friends were horsing around with Spanish moss from the trees, shown here. With the threatening international situation, Corne enlisted in the U.S. Army and received his assignment to the 178th Field Artillery Battalion. Congress declared war on December 8, 1941—Corne's birthday. (Courtesy of Imogene Davis Corne.)

At the New Georgia Islands on August 14, 1943, T.Sgt. Charles William Corne and four fellow soldiers stormed and captured a machine gun nest powerfully defended by nine enemy soldiers. T.Sgt. Charles William Corne sustained shrapnel wounds in his left leg and spent six months in a New Zealand military hospital. Corne, who married Imogene (Jean) Davis, earned the Purple Heart, Bronze Star Medal, Good Conduct Medal, American Defense Service Medal, and Asiatic Pacific Campaign Medal. (Courtesy of Imogene Davis Corne.)

Taking part in the operations on Bougainville was the 3rd Marine Division. A member of this unit was Sgt. Robert A. Owens, son of Mary Owens of Arcadia. When Robert valiantly died in battle, his parents declined to attend ceremonies in Washington D.C., even at President Harry S. Truman's request. Instead, the Medal of Honor was presented to Robert's family and friends at the Cannons Campground homestead. Sergeant Owens was one of fewer than 500 recipients of the Medal of Honor during World War II; 16 million served in the military during this time. (Courtesy of the U.S. government.)

The citation delivered by U.S. Marine Corps Maj. Gen. Clayton B. Vogel read:

During extremely hazardous operations at Cape Torokins, Bougainville, elements of Sergeant Owens's division were forced to pass within a range of 75-mm gun . . . The Marines were suffering heavy casualties . . . The success of the entire operation was threatened. Sergeant Owens unhesitatingly determined to charge the gun . . . he immediately charged into the mouth of the steadily firing cannon and entered the emplacement through the fire port, driving the gun crew out the rear door and ensuring their destruction before he himself was mortally wounded. Indomitable and aggressive in the face of certain death, Sergeant Owens . . . contributed immeasurably to the success of the vital landing operations. Sergeant Owens's conduct throughout reflects the highest credit upon himself and the United States Naval Services. He gave his life for his country [November 1, 1943].

Pvt. 1st Class Frank Hilliard Rice was a fire controlman in the 3rd Division of the U.S. Marine Corps Field Artillery from November 5, 1943, until December 15, 1943, on Bougainville Island. During his time in the U.S. Marine Corps, Rice participated in action against the enemy at Bougainville, Solomon Islands. At Guam, Marianas Islands, he was cited for volunteering to help remove the wounded from a dangerous area to the battalion aid station over a route subjected to enemy fire. (Courtesy of Jean P. Rice.)

In a brutal battle in November 1943, the U.S. Marine Corps defeated and occupied the coral atoll of Tarawa. This battle helped the U.S. Navy and the U.S. Marine Corps to develop techniques and tactics that they could use with increasing expertise in the conquests to come. Among the U.S. Marines who landed on Tarawa was Cpl. Harold Victor Conwell, a military policeman who suffered shrapnel wounds in the leg and hand. This made him one of the 3,300 casualties of the invasion. Out of approximately 4,900 Japanese on the island, fewer than 150 survived. (Courtesy of Betty J. Ray.)

Capt. Boyce V. Hawkins was in the U.S. Army Military Police. Hawkins was at the replacement training center in California, where he trained troops for two and a half years. (Courtesy of Boyce V. Hawkins.)

Hawkins's service overseas was in the China Burma India (CBI) Theatre. He served as chief military police officer in Chungking, China. He remembers seeing Generalissimo Chiang Kai-shek, the Nationalist Chinese leader, many times. Hawkins, who ended the war in charge of Japanese POWs in Shanghai, China, retired as a colonel after 30 years of military service. (Courtesy of Boyce V. Hawkins.)

Pvt. 1st Class Claude Jackson Toney Jr., 22nd Marine Battalion, participated in operations in Kwajalein, Eniwetok Atoll, Marshall Islands, and in the assault and capture of Guam, Marianas Islands. Toney served as a general clerk in his unit. Pictured with four of his comrades is C.J. Toney Jr., third from left. (Courtesy of C.J. Toney Jr. and Rev. Thomas C. Moore.)

Sgt. John W. Stevenson participated in the invasion of Saipan with the 27th Infantry Division, "New York." Later, Sergeant Stevenson engaged also in operations at Okinawa and received the Asiatic-Pacific Campaign Medal with two Bronze Service Stars. Stevenson retired from Converse College after a distinguished career as chair of the English department. (Courtesy of John W. Stevenson.)

On Angaur, Palau Island, the chaplains hold the first Sunday religious services for the troops of the victorious 81st Division, the "Wildcats." (Courtesy of Alice Inez Cummins and the Office of the Chaplain, 2nd Army, Baltimore, Maryland.)

Serving in the liberation of the Philippines was S.Sgt. Paul Barney Dobbins, Headquarters Battery, 246th Field Artillery Battalion. For his services, he received the American Defense Service Medal, the Asiatic Pacific Campaign Medal with three Bronze Services Stars, the Philippine Liberation Ribbon with one Bronze Service Star, the Good Conduct Medal, and the Honorable Discharge Medal. (Courtesy of the family of Paul Barney Dobbins and of Rev. Thomas C. Moore.)

T5g. Charles S. Vassy, Headquarters Company, 1st Battalion, 186th Infantry, 41st Division, "Sunset," served as a panel and code clerk, deciphering and enciphering messages for his unit. For his services in Papua, New Guinea, and the Southern Philippines, he earned the Combat Infantryman's Badge, the Asiatic Pacific Campaign Medal with three Bronze Services Stars, the Philippine Liberation Ribbon with one Bronze Service Star, and the Good Conduct Medal. (Courtesy of Mrs. Charles S. [Charlotte] Vassy.)

S.Sgt. Thell Wayne "T.W." Jones, 3018th Ordnance B Engineer REB Company and 141st Ordnance B Auto Maintenance Battalion, served as an automobile mechanic. His campaigns included New Guinea, Luzon, and the Philippines. Jones remembers well being sergeant of the guard in Manila the night the men heard of the Japanese capitulation. A "90-Day Wonder" came to Sergeant Jones in dismay. "Sergeant, what are we going to do? The men are shouting, shooting their weapons in the air, and drinking." Jones replied, "Nothing, sir. The men are celebrating. Leave them alone." His awards are the Good Conduct Medal, American Campaign Medal, Asiatic-Pacific Campaign Medal with two Bronze Service Stars, World War II Victory Medal, Philippine Liberation Ribbon with one Bronze Service Star, and Honorable Service Lapel Button World War II. (Courtesy of T.W. Jones.)

Sgt. Marion L. Chapman, Headquarters Squadron, 5th Bomber Command, was a high-speed radio operator in a signal detachment. During operations near Tacloban, Leyte, he received assignment to an air-sea rescue boat named "Miss Lizzie." Japanese planes bombed and strafed by the crash boat in January 1945. For his services, Sergeant Chapman earned the Asiatic-Pacific Campaign Medal with three Bronze Service Stars, the Philippine Liberation Medal with two Bronze Service Stars, the American Service Medal, the World War II Victory Medal, and the Good Conduct Medal. (Courtesy of Susan Atkins.)

S.Sgt. Donald F. Rogers, Company A, 799th Military Police Battalion, received the assignment of providing security for Gen. Douglas A. MacArthur and family during the general's return to the Philippines. Sergeant Rogers earned the Asiatic-Pacific Campaign Medal with one Bronze Service Star, the World War II Victory Medal, and the Good Conduct Medal; his unit received the Meritorious Unit Award. His comment about Australia was, "Beautiful! I would love to go back!" (Courtesy of Donald F. Rogers.)

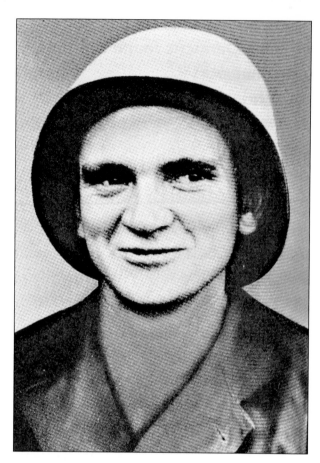

Pvt. 1st Class Thomas E. Atkins, Company A, 127th Infantry Regiment, 32nd Infantry Division, was one of two Spartanburg County boys to receive the highest military commendation: the Medal of Honor. Atkins died on September 15, 1999, and is buried in the cemetery of Fellowship Baptist Church in Inman, South Carolina. He was survived by his wife Vivian; four sons: Bobby, Ansel, Allen (Inman), and Doug (Campobello); his daughter, Frances Crocker of Inman; two brothers: Clyde (Chesnee) and Hollis (Oakbridge, Georgia); and two sisters: Lula Guffey (Duncan) and Pauline Mills (Inman). (Courtesy of U.S. Army.)

This Campobello native, his citation reads, accounted for at least 14 enemy soldiers when he "fought gallantly on the Villa Verde Trail, Luzon, Philippine Islands. With two companions he occupied a position on a ridge outside the perimeter defense established by the 1st Platoon on a high hill . . . two companies of Japanese attacked with rifle and machine gun fire, grenades, TNT charges, and land mines, severely wounding Atkins and killing his two companions. Despite the intense hostile fire and pain from his deep wound, he held his ground and returned heavy fire. After the attack was repulsed, he remained in his precarious position to repel amy subsequent assaults instead of returning to the American lines for medical treatment. An enemy machine gun, set up within 20 yards of his foxhole, vainly attempted to drive him off or silence his gun. The Japanese repeatedly made fierce attacks, but for four hours, Pfc. Atkins determinedly remained in his fox hole, bearing the brunt of each assault and maintaining steady and accurate fire until each charge was repulsed. At 7 a.m., 13 enemy dead lay in front of his position; he had fired 400 rounds, all he and his dead companions possessed, and had used three rifles until each had jammed too badly for further operation. He withdrew during a lull to secure a rifle and more ammunition, and was persuaded to remain for medical treatment. While waiting, he saw a Japanese within the perimeter and, seizing a nearby rifle, killed him. A few minutes later, while lying on a litter, he discovered an enemy group moving up behind the platoon's lines. Despite his severe wound, he sat up, delivered heavy rifle fire against the group, and forced them to withdraw. Pfc. Atkins's superb bravery and his fearless determination to hold his post against the main force of repeated enemy attacks, even though painfully wounded, were major factors in enabling his comrades to maintain their lines against a numerically superior force." (Courtesy of U.S. Army)

Six

EUROPEAN CAMPAIGNS (1944)
D-DAY, LIBERATION OF FRANCE, ARDENNES

In the European Theater, years of training and preparation achieved culmination with the massive Normandy invasion; Gen. Dwight David Eisenhower, Supreme Allied Commander, directed this "Great Crusade." After breaking out of the beachheads, Allied forces pursued the remnants of the defeated German Army back to the borders of the Fatherland. Regrouping, the Nazis staged a desperate and ultimately futile counterattack: the Ardennes Offensive.

On the night of June 5, 1944, American paratroopers of the 82nd and 101st Airborne Divisions parachuted from C-47 transport planes. Their landing zones were behind the Utah and Omaha beaches of Normandy, France. Following close behind these C-47s were *Waco* and *Horsa* gliders transporting glider-borne infantry, artillery, and communications equipment. Pictured are CG-4A *Waco* gliders. (Courtesy of William B. Foster Sr.)

Second Lt. Andrew L. Bates (first on left, standing) was piloting a *Horsa* glider towed by a C-47. They took off from Bottsford, England, at approximately 8:00 p.m. During the three-hour crossing, Bates and his co-pilot Flight Officer David L. Clark (first on left, front row) had a smooth flight. They were transporting a jeep, a trailer loaded with ammunition, and six members of the 82nd Airborne, "the All American." Gliding at 400 feet across the Cotentin Coast, Bates had only four minutes to find his landing zone near Ste. Mere Eglise. Dodging flak, Bates acquired his landing target. (Courtesy of Andrew L. Bates.)

Second Lieutenant Bates, 79th Squadron, 436th Group, IX Troop Carrier Command, recalled, "There was only one problem. The field was too short." The glider came to rest on top of a hedgerow. One of the paratroopers died in the 60-mile-per-hour landing and subsequent crash, Bates suffered a knee injury, and the co-pilot also sustained injury. Army medics evacuated the injured back to Utah Beach. Bates ended up in a hospital in Oxford, England. Clark received treatment in a hospital in Wales. Fifty years later, they were re-united for a D-Day Observance. (Courtesy of Andrew L. Bates.)

Performing another role in this "Big Show" was Flight Officer William B. Foster Sr., 89th Squadron, 438th Group, IX Troop Carrier Command. Piloting his *Waco* CG-4A glider, Foster was transporting a jeep trailer, the regimental sergeant major, and three enlisted men. The glider was following the regimental commander's aircraft with a landing zone near Ste. Mere Eglise. After landing, the aircrews guarded German prisoners captured during the invasion. Foster participated in all major airborne operations in Europe during World War II. His commendations include the Air Medal with three Oak Leaf Clusters; his unit received the Presidential Unit Citation. (Courtesy of William B. Foster Sr.)

The morning of June 6 found British troops landing at Gold Beach and Sword Beach, Canadian troops at Juno Beach, and the American troops at Utah and Omaha Beaches. James Carroll Sullivan, 29th Division, "Blue and Gray," recalls in 1999 to a group of Gable Middle School students, "I came across to Omaha Beach from England on a Landing Craft Tank. There was one vehicle on it and a platoon of men. It was rough and stormy when we got to the beach. You could hear the shells from our Navy ships and they would shake you up pretty good. The smoke was thick, and the Germans were pretty well fortified when we got in. You could see the boats getting hit and the people floating by you—wounded or dead—but you could not change course to pick them up." (Courtesy of the *Herald-Journal*, November 11, 2003, and Peggy Shull.)

CARROLL Sullivan

James Carroll Sullivan recalls the difficulty as the tanks tried to land in the rough water. "You could see them sinking right on the spot. It wasn't a picnic. I don't care who says they weren't scared. I was frightened." On June 17, 1944, Staff Sergeant Sullivan received shrapnel wounds from an artillery airburst that resulted in the loss of his right eye. (Courtesy of Peggy Shull and James Carroll Sullivan.)

Landing on Utah Beach was Walter M. "Bud" Moore Jr., Company D, 359th Infantry, 90th Division, "Tough Ombres." After surviving this hazardous landing, six months later, Sgt. Walter Moore and his jeep driver captured 27 German enlisted men and three officers. For his services, Moore received the Purple Heart, Combat Infantryman's Badge, Bronze Star Medal, EAME Campaign Medal with five Bronze Service Stars, World War II Victory Medal, and Good Conduct Medal. Despite his extraordinary military sacrifices, Bud Moore is best known today as a NASCAR race car owner and engineer. (Courtesy of Betty and Bud Moore.)

Frank H. Pruitt, Headquarters Company, 2nd Battalion, 120th Infantry, 30th Division, "Old Hickory," served as a staff sergeant in a communications platoon. He came ashore at Omaha Beach on D+3. His main duty was to maintain the communication lines between the frontline rifle companies. Sergeant Pruitt participated in the campaigns of Normandy, Northern France, Ardennes, the Rhineland, and Central Europe. Here he appears with his wife of one year: Florence Spitzer Pruitt. (Courtesy of Frank H. Pruitt.)

Promoted to staff sergeant August 1944, Frank Pruitt rejected a battlefield commission after the Battle of Mortain. Pruitt received the Combat Infantryman's Badge, Bronze Star with Oak Leaf Cluster, American Theater Medal, EAME Campaign Medal with Arrowheads and Battle Stars, World War II Victory Medal, Occupation Medal of Germany, croix de guerre (France), and Fourragere Unit Citation (Belgium); his unit received the Presidential Unit Citation and the Meritorious Unit Citation with cluster. (Courtesy of Frank Pruitt.)

Pvt. 1st Class Richard B. Harris, Company C, 1st Battalion, 175th Infantry, 29th Division, "Blue and Gray," came ashore on a Landing Craft Tank at Omaha Beach. He said that he "disembarked in water over my head and was machine-gunned by Germans on the beach." Here the officers of his regiment overlook German prisoners. He recalls fighting the cruel Nazi SS troops. Concussed and wounded by shrapnel from a 280 mm railway gun shell, he was unconscious for three days and woke in a hospital in Holland. For his services he earned the Purple Heart, Combat Infantryman's Badge, Silver Star Medal, EAME Campaign Medal with five Bronze Service Stars, World War II Victory Medal, Good Conduct Medal, and Honorable Discharge Medal. (Courtesy of Richard B. Harris.)

Pvt. 1st Class James D. Miller, Company A, 314th Infantry, 79th Division, "Lorraine," served as a bazooka-man. He recalls that on his first day in combat he saw two Americans lying face down in the mud in Normandy. Miller received a leg wound during his service and received the Purple Heart. For his services in the Normandy, Northern France, Ardennes, Rhineland, and Central Europe campaigns, Miller earned the Combat Infantryman's Badge, American Theater Campaign Medal, EAME Campaign Medal with four Bronze Service Stars, World War II Victory Medal, and Good Conduct Medal; his unit received the Distinguished Unit Badge. (Courtesy of James Miller.)

Cpl. Broadus W. Collins, Detachment
B, Service Battery, 196th Field Artillery
Battalion, had the duty of Wire NCO.
He participated in the Normandy,
Northern France, Rhineland, Ardennes,
and Central Europe campaigns. He
earned the EAME Campaign Medal
with five Bronze Service Stars, the
American Defense Service Medal,
and the Good Conduct Medal.
(Courtesy of Broadus W. Collins.)

Pvt. Virgil L. Barnett, Headquarters
Company, 926th Combat Signal
Battalion, landed on Omaha Beach
from a Landing Ship Tank. He recalls
"the water was red, and bodies were
everywhere. I remember stepping over
the bodies in order to walk." During the
war, he captured a German colonel and
"remembers him with his hands in the
air" before turning him over to the MPs.
He served as a truck driver during the
Normandy, Northern France, Ardennes,
and Rhineland campaigns and earned
the EAME Campaign Medal with four
Bronze Service Stars, World War II
Victory Medal, and Good Conduct
Medal. Mrs. Barnett met her husband in
the Tucapau Mill where he "drove the
dope (concession) wagon" and she had
a third-shift job. She reported that "he
tore her heart out" the first time she saw
him, and that "he still does." (Courtesy
of Mr. and Mrs. Virgil L. Barnett.)

S.Sgt. Robert Richard Burchfield, Troop B, 88th Cavalry School Squadron, was a Motor Transport NCO during the Normandy, Northern France, Ardennes, Rhineland, and Central Europe campaigns. Here he stands beside a destroyed German *Messerschmitt* 109 fighter. (Courtesy of Lois Burchfield.)

S.Sgt. Richard Burchfield earned the Combat Infantryman's Badge, Bronze Star Medal, American Theater Campaign Medal, EAME Campaign Medal with Service Star, World War II Victory Medal, and Good Conduct Medal. His unit earned the Distinguished Unit Badge. The stress of combat made it possible for soldiers to learn to rest anywhere. Here S.Sgt. Richard Burchfield has "kicked back" after his hazardous duty. (Courtesy of Lois Burchfield.)

Albert Price participated in the Normandy Campaign, where, according to his cousin Mary Pierce Edwards Hawkins, "he courageously fought and lost an eye in combat." He was a recipient of the Purple Heart and the EAME Campaign Medal. Other Price relatives who served were Jack and Robert Price. (Courtesy of Mary Price Edwards Hawkins.)

During a lull in the action, a chaplain conducts religious services for members of an infantry unit. The photo illustrates the hedgerows of the Bocage country of northwestern France. The hood of a jeep serves as a communion table for the infantrymen, who have placed their helmets and weapons within easy reach. (Courtesy of Alice Inez Cummins and the Chaplain's Office 2nd Army, Baltimore, Maryland.)

Military hospitals in England cared for the injuries suffered by Allied personnel. Pvt. 1st Class Raymond R. Henderson received assignment to the 305th Hospital Unit. His many duties included that of an ambulance driver. The wounded landed at the city of Weymouth on the English Channel and received transport to area hospitals. Henderson worked in the hospital until the end of the war. Here he poses with his wife, Leona Henderson. (Courtesy of Mike Hembree.)

Also serving in England was Capt. William C. "Cotton" Cannon, Ordnance Department, Company O, 4th Battalion. For his maintenance and preparedness of 50,000 military vehicles, Capt. William Cotton received the U.S. Army's Bronze Star Medal at U.S. General Depot G25 in England. He operated the largest vehicle distribution center in the European Theater of Operations; he accomplished this achievement with limited personnel. "By means of systematic maintenance and storage he assured that combat troops would receive thoroughly serviceable vehicles ready to take off from LCTs and LCSs on the beach. . . . Every convoy team arrived at its destined port of embarkation on time." (Courtesy of Mary Cannon.)

Pvt. Jack Phillips, Headquarters and Service Company, 85th Engineer Heavy Pontoon Battalion, served as a driver for officers in his unit in England. Pvt. Jack Phillips received the EAME Campaign Medal, the American Theater Service Ribbon, and the World War II Victory Medal. (Courtesy of Jack and Marbelle Phillips.)

To help maintain the morale of the troops overseas, the USO sponsored numerous tours of entertainers, musicians, actors, and actresses. One of these visitors was the actress Loretta Young, pictured with enthusiastic GIs. (Courtesy of Mary Cannon.)

T5g. Jesse W. Parris, 109th Port Marine Maintenance Company, served as a shipfitter; he installed and repaired pipes and plumbing as necessary in vessels in the European Theater. His decorations include the EAME Campaign Medal, the American Service Medal, the World War II Victory Medal, and the Good Conduct Medal. (Courtesy of Jesse W. Parris.)

Pvt. 1st Class Leroy Ray, Company B, 15th Infantry, 3rd Division, "Rock of the Marne," suffered serious wounds: one gunshot wound to the right elbow and two gunshot wounds to the spinal cord. These injuries occurred near Nancy, France, on November 2, 1944. For his services, he earned the Purple Heart, Combat Infantryman's Badge, Bronze Star with Oak Leaf Cluster, EAME Campaign Medal with one Bronze Service Star, and Good Conduct Medal. (Courtesy of Ronnie Ray.)

Serving in Company K, 3rd Battalion, 2nd Regiment, 5th Division, "the Red Diamonds," was Pvt. 1st Class William J. Ware. He participated in five European campaigns and earned the Purple Heart Medal with Oak Leaf Cluster, Combat Infantryman's Badge, EAME Campaign Medal with five Bronze Service Stars, American Defense Service Medal, American Campaign Medal, Occupation of Germany Medal, World War II Victory Medal, and Good Conduct Medal. Ware noted, "My life in Europe: frontline combat most every day, facing Germans, mortar barrages, 88 mm artillery, mines, rifle fire, snipers, tanks, tree bursts—DEATH." This is a photo of Private First Class Ware (left) and his friend "Shorty" (right). (Courtesy of William J. Ware.)

Cpl. Wilford Dodd, Company B, 397th Infantry, 100th Division, "Century," 7th Army, was killed in action on November 22, 1944, in the vicinity of Senones, France. He had been overseas only one month. Posthumously, he received a Bronze Star Medal for "unhesitatingly leaving his position of comparative security to repair a severed communication line. He remained at the task when he was mortally wounded by mortar and artillery fire." He was survived by his wife and a daughter he had never seen; he received the Purple Heart posthumously. (Courtesy of Mary Dodd Lyles.)

Technician William J. Kimball served with an ordnance outfit in France and the Ruhr Valley of Germany. He enlisted in 1942 and served until 1946. The duty of his unit was tank recovery. He remembers that many of the bridges were not strong enough to support the tanks and the recovery vehicles. He earned the Purple Heart, EAME Campaign Medal with two Bronze Service Stars, World War II Victory Medal, and Good Conduct Medal. Dr. Kimball served as English professor at Converse College from 1965 until his 1987 retirement. (Courtesy of Converse College and Bill Kimball.)

Sgt. Charles Tillman Johnson served as a forward artillery observer with the 109th Field Artillery Battalion, 28th Division, "Keystone," during the Battle of the Bulge. He observed the enemy between Clervaux and Bastogne and volunteered to go forward to ascertain if silhouettes seen on the skyline were enemy vehicles. From a church steeple he confirmed that they were indeed German tanks. After the war, Charles B. McDonald included Johnson in the book *A Time for Trumpets* (William Morrow Company, 1985). For his services, Johnson won the Silver Star Medal, EAME Campaign Medal with two Bronze Service Stars, Occupation Medal (Germany), American Campaign Medal, and Good Conduct Medal. (Courtesy of Betty P. Cantrell.)

Pvt. 1st Class Russell Gale Dehne, 9th Division, "Varsity," 1st Army, received his training at Camp Blanding, Florida, in the spring of 1944. Here he is participating in a bayonet drill with fellow soldier Raymond Shotts. Dehne wrote on the back of the photo, "Puttin' it on ole Shotts." Dehne served as a rifleman during the action near the Hurtgen Forest and the Siegfried Line. His granddaughter Laura Lee Corbin compiled his information. (Courtesy of Barbara Dehne Corbin.)

Dehne was wounded December 11, 1944. He earned the Purple Heart, the Combat Infantryman's Badge, the EAME with one Bronze Service Star, and the Good Conduct Medal. Although he never talked of the war, he often said the photos of his wife and daughter in his wallet brought him through the bad times. This photo shows him on furlough with his daughter Barbara; his daughter Marsha Dehne Fores was not born until 1946. (Courtesy of Barbara Dehne Corbin.)

Cpl. James Leroy Burnett, Company C, 442nd Infantry, 106th Division, "Golden Lions," served as company clerk. During the German advance, the enemy overran his unit, and he was captured on December 19, 1944. He was transported by rail to Stalag IXB, Bad Orb, Germany; for five days he was packed into a boxcar with other POWs. The Christmas meal was a piece of bread with cabbage soup. When he developed pneumonia, he received the special care of Father Cavanaugh, who helped ensure his survival. On May 12, 1945, Burnett received his liberation. He earned the Combat Infantryman's Badge, American Theater Medal, EAME Campaign Medal with two Bronze Service Stars, World War II Victory Medal, and Good Conduct Medal. (Courtesy of Mr. and Mrs. James Leroy Burnett.)

Helping to stop the German advance were the men of the 101st Airborne Division. One of these "Screaming Eagles" was Charles L. Dobbins. Dobbins suffered wounds in Belgium, and for his services, he earned the Purple Heart, the Combat Infantryman's Badge, the EAME Campaign Medal, and the Good Conduct Medal. (Courtesy of Rev. Thomas C. Moore.)

Pvt. 1st Class Harold W. Hayes, Headquarters Company, 7th Armored Division, "the Lucky Seventh," participated in the Ardennes, Northern France, Rhineland, and Central Europe campaigns. As a jeep driver, he transported men and materials on the advance from Normandy to the Baltic Sea. He earned the EAME Campaign Medal with four Bronze Service Stars and the Good Conduct Medal. Pictured with Harold W. Hayes (right) is his brother Perrin Willis Hayes (left); the two stayed together from the Mohave Desert to the Baltic. There were four in the Hayes family, and three boys were in service concurrently. (Courtesy of Harold W. Hayes.)

Pvt. 1st Class Troy Oma Edwards, 814th Tank Destroyer Battalion, entered service at the age of 34; at the age of 96 he is still articulate about his service. He and his unit saw combat during the time of the Battle of the Bulge. His narrow escapes included an incident in Holland ("where a house was blown up while I was in the basement") and "times when I had to step over the bodies of Germans and Americans lay dead side to side. We don't know what hell is, but I can tell you war is hell." He earned the EAME Campaign Medal with two Bronze Service Stars, the World War II Victory Medal, and the Good Conduct Medal. (Courtesy of Troy Oma Edwards.)

A Spartanburg family had seven sons in uniform during World War II. Bernard and Lillie Foster were proud of these fine young men, all of whom returned at war's end. This photograph, taken shortly after the end of the war, shows, from left to right, the Foster brothers and brothers-in-law: (front row) U.S. Army Cpt. William Player Law (brother-in-law); U.S. Army Lt. Col. Bernard Foster Jr., who served in the Pentagon throughout the war; U.S. Army Air Forces Col. Donald Calvin Foster, who served in the Mediterranean Theater; (back row) U.S. Army Capt. Julian Allen Foster, who served in the South Pacific; U.S. Navy Cmdr. Shelby Clark (brother-in-law); U.S. Army Lt. Philip Francis Foster; U.S. Army Maj. Ralph Veazey Foster, who served in the Mediterranean Theater; U.S. Navy Lt. Howard Gordon Foster, a pilot on the USS *Hancock*; U.S. Navy Lt. (jg) William Edwin Foster, who received his commission after the war. It is difficult for us to imagine the fear that these parents must have felt whenever they heard a knock on the door. (Courtesy of Mr. and Mrs. Shelby Clark.)

Seven

A Two-Ocean Navy (1941–1945)

Atlantic and Pacific

The naval battle in the Atlantic Ocean presented the U.S. Atlantic Fleet with the challenge of helping the United Kingdom's Royal Navy to defeat the German submarine menace. Defeat of the U-boats would allow the Allies to move the vital supplies and the millions of troops across the seas—vital steps for the defeat of Adolf Hitler. These sailors overcame the hidden dangers of the "wolf packs" and the fierce storms of the North Atlantic Ocean. The navy's ultimate success freed Europe from the grasp of the odious tyrant.

After the attack on Pearl Harbor, the U.S. Pacific Fleet faced the well-trained and hard-fighting Imperial Fleet of the Japanese Empire. Ranging across the vast ocean were ships that spanned the entire inventory of the American Navy. Using every type of ship—from smallest landing craft to the far-ranging carrier task forces—the U.S. Navy battled the implacable foe. By September 1945, the fleet, under command of fighting admirals like William F. Halsey Jr., Raymond A. Spruance, and Marc A. Mitscher, had utterly defeated the proud Japanese. With the surrender in Tokyo Bay, the U.S. Navy reached a pinnacle of power, which it still maintains today.

The USS *Guam*, a large cruiser, participated in the Pacific raids of 1945 and the invasion of Okinawa. This ship and its sister USS *Alaska* helped supply anti-aircraft protection for the fast carrier task forces of Vice Admirals Halsey and Spruance. (Courtesy of John N. George Jr.)

The U.S. Merchant Marines used countless ships to move supplies and men worldwide during the war. The U.S. Navy supplied sailors, like Gunners Mate 3rd Class J.T. Wilburn Hembree, for the gun crews on these vessels. Hembree entered service on August 27, 1942, and took the first train ride of his life to Columbia, South Carolina. Later, when he arrived in Norfolk, Virginia, the boys in the barracks hollered, "You'll be sorry!" Hembree said, "Heck! I already was!" He would serve on the SS *Seminole*, the SS *Agwiprince*, the SS *Peale*, and the SS *George P. McKay*. The SS *Peale* transported 300 men of the 2nd Division on shore at Normandy. (Courtesy of Mike Hembree.)

Lt. Oscar M. Spencer retired from the U.S. Navy after 25 years of service. He served aboard the USS *Savannah* and the USS *O'Bannon*. (Courtesy of Barbara A. Morgan.)

Brothers Oscar M. and John H. Spencer served aboard the USS *Savannah*, which participated in the invasion of Salerno, Italy, in 1943. During the action, a German bomb struck the light cruiser and killed approximately 200 sailors. After this incident, Ens. Oscar M. Spencer requested transfer so he and his brother would not be serving on the same vessel. Oscar received assignment to the USS *O'Bannon*; John remained aboard the *Savannah* and retired as a warrant officer after 20 years. (Courtesy of Barbara A. Morgan.)

Lt. Robert L. Stoddard enlisted in the U.S. Navy on February 1, 1942. Commissioned from the V-7 Program in June 1942, he served aboard the USS *Long Island* and saw action in both the Atlantic and the Pacific. He also served aboard the USS *Prince William* and saw service in the Pacific until April 1, 1944. He attended radar training school until June 1944. Stoddard was a plank owner of the large cruiser USS *Guam* and served in the radar and gunnery. The *Guam* saw action off the coasts of Japan, Okinawa, and China. The Honorable Robert L. Stoddard is perhaps best remembered in Spartanburg County for his service as Spartanburg mayor. (Courtesy of Robert L. Stoddard.)

Serving aboard the USS *Guam* as an anti-aircraft machine gun crewman was Corp. John N. George Jr. of the U.S. Marine Corps. He served on the ship's 4th Division, Port 20 mm guns and received the American Campaign Medal, the Asiatic-Pacific Campaign Medal, two Bronze Service Stars, the Japan Occupation Medal, the China Service Medal, the World War II Victory Medal, and the Philippine Liberation Ribbon. John N. George was one of 18 South Carolinians, including Robert Stoddard, to serve aboard the USS *Guam*. (Courtesy of John N. George Jr.)

Chief PO Harold Davis served from July 1940 until May 1946. His ships included the USS *Whitney* and the USS *Birmingham*, where he served as chief pay clerk. The crew of the *Birmingham* sustained major casualties when trying to extinguish the fires on the USS *Princeton*, which had exploded as a result of a Japanese bomb during the Battle of Leyte in October 1944, and the bomb showered the deck of the *Birmingham* with burning fuel and debris. Davis received the Good Conduct Medal, American Defense Service Medal with Bronze Service Star, Asiatic Pacific Campaign Medal with seven Bronze Services Stars, Philippine Liberation Ribbon with Service Star, World War II Victory Medal, and Honorable Discharge Lapel Pin. Davis retired as chief warrant officer. (Courtesy of Mrs. Harold [Nena] Davis.)

Seaman 1st Class Max Morris Robbins
was a Special Artificer (Special Devices) in
the U.S. Navy. Robbins, who used a
Link Trainer to instruct aviators at the
U.S. Naval Air Station in San Diego,
California, was the son of Mr. and Mrs.
L.B. Robbins of Rutherfordton and
Caroleen, North Carolina. After the war,
Robbins was best known as the principal
of Spartanburg High School. (Courtesy
of Mrs. Max [Wanda] Robbins.)

Yeoman 2nd Class Joe William McCraw served aboard the USS *John Hood*, a destroyer that
operated in the North Pacific Ocean while based in the Aleutian Islands, Alaska. The ship
conducted bombardments of the Kurile Islands from November 1944 until August 1945.
McCraw also served in the occupation of Japan. For his services, he earned the American
Theater Campaign Medal, the Asiatic Pacific Campaign Medal with one Bronze Services Star,
and the World War II Victory Medal. This photo shows McCraw (middle, back row) with the
other yeomen of the USS *John Hood*. (Courtesy of Joe William McCraw.)

Yeoman Chief PO Maurice W. Burgess became a plank owner of the USS *Rombach* when the destroyer escort was launched from Orange, Texas. The *Rombach* served in the Pacific area for the entire war. For his services, he received the American Defense Service Medal, the American Theater Campaign Medal, the Asiatic Pacific Campaign Medal, the World War II Victory Medal, the Good Conduct Medal, and the Honorable Discharge Medal. (Courtesy of Maurice W. Burgess.)

Electrician's Mate 2nd Class Richard Wayne Hendrix served aboard the USS *Franklin* and the USS *Bennington,* both Essex class aircraft carriers. Here he is pictured with the original ship's bell from the *Franklin*. He enlisted in the navy on June 2, 1941, six months before Pearl Harbor. His brother William E. Hendrix Jr. enlisted in the U.S. Army Air Corps on March 19, 1941; their father (W.E. Hendrix Sr.) served in both World War I and World War II. (Courtesy of Richard W. Hendrix.)

Electrician's Mate 2nd Class Richard Wayne Hendrix was on the *Bennington* (pictured above) when it sustained a hit by a kamikaze off the coast of Okinawa in the spring of 1945. Hendrix participated in operations in Saipan, Tinian, Leyte, Iwo Jima, and Okinawa. He earned the American Defense Service Medal, the American Theater Campaign Medal, the Asiatic Pacific Campaign Medal with five Bronze Services Stars, the World War II Victory Medal, the Good Conduct Medal, and the Honorable Discharge Medal. (Courtesy of Richard W. Hendrix.)

Fire Controlman 1st Class Whitner Livingston Griffin Jr. served aboard the USS *Indiana* in the gunnery department. He was in charge of a secondary plotting room just prior to the invasion of Saipan in June 1944. At www. geocities.com/ bb58.geo/remembrances/ remembrances1.html, Griffin tells of maintaining and repairing the fire control computers. He received the Combat Action Ribbon, the American Theater Campaign Medal, the Asiatic-Pacific Campaign Medal with nine Bronze Service Stars, the World War II Victory Medal, and the Good Conduct Medal. (Courtesy of Whitner Livingston Griffin Jr.)

Lt. (jg) Thomas Edward Langston served aboard the USS *Wasatch*. The *Wasatch* was an amphibious force flagship for 7th Fleet. Admiral Thomas C. Kinkaid was in charge of the naval forces when General MacArthur returned to Leyte, Philippines, on October 20, 1944. Langston served also at the invasions of Luzon, Mindanao, and Balikpapan, Borneo. (Courtesy of Golda Langston.)

Radioman 3rd Class Jacob Thornwell "Thorny" Sill served aboard the ill-fated USS *Gambier Bay*. On October 24, 1944, battleships and cruisers from the Imperial Japanese fleet surprised the *Gambier Bay* and several other small escort carriers off Samar, Philippine Islands. During the desperate battle that ensued, the escort carriers attempted to flee for survival. After three Japanese cruisers riddled the *Gambier Bay*, the ship capsized and sank. Although he suffered face wounds, Sill survived and spent 48–50 agonizing hours in the shark-infested waters. He earned the Purple Heart, American Area Campaign Medal, Asiatic-Pacific Campaign Medal with five Bronze Service Stars, EAME Campaign Medal, Philippine Liberation Ribbon, World War II Victory Medal, and Good Conduct Medal; his unit received the Presidential Unit Citation. (Courtesy of Thorny Sill.)

Seaman 1st Class Geraldine Marie Houk Sill met her husband at the North Island Naval Base in San Diego. She served as teletype operator. The duration of her duty was about one and a half years. After the war, she served as a switchboard operator at Converse College in Spartanburg. (Courtesy of Geraldine Marie Houk Sill.)

U.S. Navy Lt. William L. Ball Jr. served as a chaplain with the 93rd Naval Construction Battalion in the Philippines. Chaplain Ball always arranged his worship services so that the men faced the ocean. The services helped to maintain morale. The men, who were older and usually had families at home, often decorated the chapel with murals. A special memory was a USO visit from Bob Hope, Jerry Colonna, and Frances Langford. The men made a stage for Hope and his company; they named the stage "Hollywood and Vine." After the war, Ball married Bessie Rice Ball, who had toured with a USO group at the end of the war. (Courtesy of Mrs. William L. [Bessie] Ball Jr.)

For his services, U.S. Navy Lt. William L. Ball Jr. received the American Theater Campaign Medal, the Asiatic-Pacific Campaign Medal with two Bronze Service Stars, the Philippine Liberation Medal, the World War II Victory Medal, and the Honorable Discharge Medal. He married Bessie Rice and served both Fernwood Baptist Church and First Baptist Church in Spartanburg, South Carolina. Their son Will later served as Secretary of the Navy and another son, David, became nationally known as a country entertainer. The community also regards highly their daughter and their other two sons. (Courtesy of Mrs. William L. [Bessie] Ball Jr.)

Second Class PO Ralph Vernon Atkins (fourth row, first on left) served as a cook on LST 270. He and his ship participated in five campaigns in 1944 and 1945. Pictured is the crew of the LST 270. Without these unheralded ships, the invasions of the Pacific Islands would never have been successful. Transporting tanks, heavy equipment, ammunition, and supplies, they were vital to the fleet. (Courtesy of Mrs. Ralph Vernon [Madge] Atkins.)

For his services, 2nd Class PO Ralph Vernon Atkins earned the American Theater Campaign Medal, the Asiatic-Pacific Campaign Medal with three Bronze Service Stars, and the Good Conduct Medal. He received his discharge at Norfolk, Virginia, in 1945. (Courtesy of Mrs. Ralph Vernon [Madge] Atkins.)

Seaman 2nd Class Walter Lamar Pridgeon served at the Naval Training Center, Bainbridge, Maryland. After the war, he went to work for Southern Bell Telephone Company and became an active member of Fernwood Baptist Church. For his wartime services, he earned the American Theater Campaign Medal, the World War II Victory Medal, the Good Conduct Medal, and the Honorable Discharge Medal. (Courtesy of Walter Lamar Pridgeon.)

Ernest D. "Runt" Foster entered the service on February 16, 1942. He served overseas in the U.S. Navy for 20 months as a pharmacist's mate 2nd class. He earned the Asiatic-Pacific Campaign Medal, the Good Conduct Medal, and the Honorable Discharge Medal. (Courtesy of Rev. Thomas C. Moore.)

Motor Machinist's Mate 1st Class Lewis M. Gainey served in the U.S. Navy aboard the fleet ocean tug USS *Abnaki*. In June 1944, the *Abnaki* had the duty of towing the captured German U-505 back to Norfolk, Virginia. He received the American Campaign Medal and the Asiatic-Pacific Campaign Medal. (Courtesy of Joseph R. Gainey.)

Seaman 1st Class Ray Earl Thompson served aboard the LST 543. This LST 543 participated in the assault and occupation of Okinawa and in the occupation duties related to the Far East and China until 1946. Thompson received the American Theater Campaign Medal, the Asiatic-Pacific Campaign Medal with one Bronze Service Star, the Philippine Liberation Ribbon, and the World War II Victory Medal. (Courtesy of Ray Earl Thompson.)

Almost all service personnel kept a memento of their time in service. First Class Ray Earl Thompson and the crew of the LST 543 signed a two-dollar bill on August 24, 1944, as a remembrance of their time in the service together. Thompson preserved the cherished item and never spent it. (Courtesy of Ray Earl Thompson.)

Alice Adelia Suiter served as a WAVE in the U.S. Navy during World War II and earned the rank of lieutenant junior grade. Her duties included recruiting in Columbia, South Carolina; on the West Coast, she scheduled entertainers for service personnel. From 1960 until 1983 when she retired, Suiter served as dean of admissions and director of financial aid at Converse College. (Courtesy of Converse College and James Harrison, Mickel Archives.)

Water Tender 2nd Class Charles William Shehan served aboard LST 928, which became the USS *Cameron*. He earned the American Area Campaign Medal, the Asiatic-Pacific Campaign Medal with one Bronze Service Star, the World War II Victory Medal, and an Honorable Discharge Medal. (Courtesy of Jackie Campbell Shehan and Meg Goodwin Cooksey.)

Jackie Campbell Shehan and Water Tender 2nd Class Charles William Shehan enjoyed some time together in Tijuana, Mexico, while he was on leave. (Courtesy of Jackie Campbell Shehan and Meg Goodwin Cooksey.)

The light aircraft carrier USS *Cowpens* received its name in commemoration of the Battle of Cowpens, the Revolutionary War battle of January 17, 1781. The launching was from the Camden Shipyards, Philadelphia, on January 17, 1943—the 162nd anniversary of the battle. "*The Mighty Moo*" earned 12 Battle Stars for participation in operations at Kwajalein, New Guinea, Palau, Leyte Gulf, Iwo Jima, and other actions and raids; it was present at the Japanese surrender in Tokyo Bay, September 1945. James M. Walker photographed the *Cowpens* mural, painted by Keith Emory, June 11, 1994, on the side of Bogan's Auto Parts on 401 Battleground Road and just outside the town of Cowpens, South Carolina. (Courtesy of Don Bogan.)

At war's end, Mrs. Daisy Lemons of Whitney, South Carolina, humbly thanked her God for the safe delivery of her seven sons and a son-in-law. On the wall behind her chair is a composite photo of, from left to right: Lt. (jg) Joseph Leon Lemons, fireman 1st class; Homer D. Lemons, radioman 2nd class; James H. Lemons, mailman 3rd class; Marion A. Lemons, storekeeper 3rd class; George Allen Lemons and Seaman 1st Class Albert M. Lemons (twins); and Seaman 2nd Class Ernest Elvon Lemons. (Courtesy of the *Herald-Journal*.)

Eight

Prevailing in Europe (1945)
Germany, the Rhineland,

the Surrender

The year 1945 began with the defeat of the last German counter-offensive in the west. With the crossing of the Rhine River in March 1945, the Allies advanced across Germany to the Elbe River. In the east, the Soviet Union's Red Army stood poised on the Oder River to attack Berlin.

Pvt. 1st Class Joe Hill Cantrell Jr., 127th Field Artillery Battalion, 35th Infantry Division, "Santa Fe," served as a surgical technician and medic. Hill (third from left, wearing a Red Cross helmet) recalled having to retrieve wounded men from a mine field and meeting in Holland a family to whom he still writes. For his services, he earned the EAME Campaign Medal with five Bronze Service Stars, the World War II Victory Medal, the Good Conduct Medal, and the Honorable Discharge Pin. (Courtesy of Joe Hill Cantrell.)

Pvt. 1st Class John R. Caldwell, Cannon Company, 137th Infantry, 35th Division, "Santa Fe," was a light artillery gun crewman. He remembered most that he defended a Dutch family and helped to teach a little Dutch girl (age six or seven) to walk. The family gave him her pair of wooden shoes. For his service, he received the EAME Campaign Medal, the Good Conduct Medal, and the Honorable Discharge Pin. (Courtesy of Lottie T. Caldwell.)

S.Sgt. Roy L. Hall, 78th Signal Company, 78th Infantry Division, "the Lightning Division," was a field lineman. His division was among the first to cross the Rhine River at Remagen on the Ludendorff Railway Bridge. This 1945 photograph shows Sgt. Victor Eash with guitar and Staff Sergeant Hall with their jeep in Germany. Wire at the back of the jeep, boxes on the front fenders, wire cutters on the front bumper, and other equipment indicate that the American Army made good use of the jeep. (Courtesy of Roy L. Hall.)

Before going overseas, S.Sgt. Roy L. Hall also served at San Juan, Puerto Rico; Ponce, Puerto Rico; and New Orleans, Louisiana. He went to England before going to France and Germany. He recalls one night when they met a bus on the "wrong side" of the road in England. Here he (center) poses with two of his fellow sergeants. For his services, he earned the EAME Campaign Medal with three Bronze Service Stars, the American Theater Campaign Medal, the American Defense Service Medal, and the Good Conduct Medal. (Courtesy of Roy L. Hall.)

Lt. Haskell C. Cook served as an 81 mm mortar platoon leader in the 387th Regiment, 97th Infantry Division, participating in operations in the Ruhr Valley of Germany. He ended the war with the 3rd Army in Czechoslovakia. After the war's end in Europe, he served in the occupation forces in Japan. He qualified as a paratrooper in the 11th Airborne Division and retired from the Army Reserves as lieutenant colonel. He earned the EAME Campaign Medal with two Bronze Service Stars, World War II Victory Medal, Japan Occupation Medal, and Honorable Discharge Pin. (Courtesy of Haskell C. Cook.)

Pvt. 1st Class Fred Hawkins, Company A, 289th Infantry Regiment, 75th Division, was a Browning Automatic rifleman. His civilian occupation was as a "switchman" for the Southern Railway. He received the Bronze Star on April 9, 1945, for his meritorious conduct, as well as the EAME Campaign Medal and the World War II Victory Medal. Fred is pictured in France. (Courtesy of Mary E. Hawkins.)

Pvt. 1st Class Robert E. Le Brun, Company A, 304th Infantry Regiment, 76th Division, participated in the Ardennes, Rhineland, and Central Europe campaigns. He earned the Bronze Star Medal, the Combat Infantryman's Badge, the EAME Campaign Medal with three Bronze Service Stars, the American Theater Campaign Medal, the World War II Victory Medal, the German Occupation Medal, the Good Conduct Medal, and the Honorable Discharge Pin. (Courtesy of Robert E. Le Brun.)

T5g. James C. Floyd, Company A, 407th Infantry, 102nd Division, "Ozarks," was wounded on March 29, 1945, in Germany and again on April 18, 1945. He helped deliver supplies with the "Red Ball Express" from La Havre to Paris before serving as a jeep driver transporting mortar shells to the front. On one occasion, he carried 8 men in his jeep to the hospital 13 miles away; then he rested for a few minutes before his next assignment. For his services, he earned a Purple Heart with an Oak Leaf Cluster. (Courtesy of James C. Floyd.)

S.Sgt. Mack R. Floyd (right), Company M, 26th Infantry, 1st Infantry Division, "the Big Red One," went ashore on D-Day and also participated in the Battle of Hurtgen Forest. His brother was James C. Floyd (left). He earned the Purple Heart and the EAME Campaign Medal with five Bronze Service Stars. Mack Floyd passed away in 1990. (Courtesy of James C. Floyd, probably from *The Spartanburg Herald*.)

Walter C. Garrett, Headquarters Company, 1st Battalion, 334th Infantry, 84th Division, "Railsplitters," participated in the Ardennes, Rhineland, and Central Europe campaigns. He recalls at the end of the war the Germans were using boys as young as 14 or 15 as soldiers. Garrett (fourth from left) was present with his battalion commander at the capture of German Colonel von Witzleben and his field wife near the Elbe River. (Courtesy of Walter C. Garrett.)

After 21 years, 7 months, and 3 days, Garrett retired as master sergeant. His awards include the Bronze Star Medal, the Combat Infantryman's Badge, the American Theater Campaign Medal, the EAME Campaign Medal with three Bronze Service Stars, the World War II Victory Medal, the Good Conduct Medal, and the Honorable Discharge Pin. His unit received the Presidential Unit Citation. (Courtesy of Walter C. Garrett.)

Pvt. 1st Class Johnie R. Parris, Troop B, 121st Cavalry Reconnaissance Squadron, served as a truck driver during the Normandy, Northern France, Rhineland, and Central Europe campaigns. For his services, he received the American Theater Campaign Medal, the EAME Campaign Medal with four Bronze Service Stars, and the Good Conduct Medal. (Courtesy of Mrs. James Fred Casey Jr.)

Sgt. W. Paul Skelton Sr., 2nd Battalion, 410th Infantry Regiment, 103rd Division, "Cactus," served in the Rhone Valley, Ardennes, and Rhineland campaigns. He earned the Purple Heart Medal, the Silver Star Medal, Bronze Star Medal, the Combat Infantryman's Badge, the EAME Campaign Medal with three Bronze Service Stars, and the World War II Victory Medal. (Courtesy of W. Paul Skelton Sr.)

Sgt. W. Paul Skelton Sr. is pictured with his future wife, Nancy, in Spartanburg. Spartanburg perhaps knows Paul best for his work as a CPA, his service to Fernwood Baptist Church, and his devotion to his family. (Courtesy of W. Paul Skelton Sr.)

T5g. Charles Edgar Edwards, 4244th Quartermaster Service Company, served as mail clerk. He participated in the Rhineland and Central Europe campaigns. He earned the American Theater Campaign Medal, the EAME Campaign Medal with two Bronze Service Stars, the World War II Victory Medal, and the Good Conduct Medal. (Courtesy of Mary Price Edwards Hawkins.)

S.Sgt. Robert F. Haynie, 144th Ordnance Motor Vehicle Assembly Company, participated in Operation PAPERCLIP, meaning that his unit was responsible for shipping from the Dora-Nordhausen Assembly Plant to Antwerp, Belgium, all items used to launch the V-2 rocket. He recalled with pride how he recovered a launch control panel in the presence of German scientist Werner von Braun. Here he poses before the tail section of a V-2 (A-4) rocket. (Courtesy of Robert F. Haynie.)

For his services, S.Sgt. Robert F. Haynie earned the EAME Campaign Medal with four Bronze Service Stars, the World War II Victory Medal, and the Good Conduct Medal; his unit received the Meritorious Unit Award. Here he perches on the V-2 (A-4) rocket. (Courtesy of Robert F. Haynie.)

Pvt. Raymond McCurry, 92nd Cavalry Reconnaissance Squadron, 12th Armored Division, "Hellcats," participated in the Rhineland and Central Europe campaigns. He recalled seeing General Patton several times and "was amazed at how Patton would put himself in harm's way." In a night battle, Raymond was wounded by artillery fire in the left arm. He was evacuated to Glasgow, Scotland, and the United States. Much of his treatment took place in Augusta, Georgia. For his services, he earned the Purple Heart, the EAME Campaign Medal, and the Good Conduct Medal. (Courtesy of Mrs. James Fred Casey; information from Vickie Casey Fowler and Raymond McCurry.)

Pvt. Neubert McCurry completed his basic training as a tank mechanic in Florida. Assigned to an ordnance unit, he served in France and Germany, as did his brother Raymond. Neubert, however, did not see combat. (Courtesy of Mrs. James Fred Casey.)

Pvt. James Luther Lancaster, 1st Platoon, C Battery, 10th AARTC, served as a crewman on a 90 mm gun. At the time of his induction (1944), he had six children and a wife at home. His awards included the Good Conduct Medal, the American Campaign Service Medal, the EAME Campaign Medal, and the World War II Victory Medal. This photo of Lancaster and his wife, Ruth, shows him on leave before his deployment. (Courtesy of Harold L. Lancaster.)

Jewish soldiers conducted religious services in Schloss Rheydt, Mönchengladbach, Germany. Nazi Propaganda Minister Dr. Joseph Paul Goebbels owned the castle, which the U.S. forces had liberated. The service is in memory of the Jewish boys lost in the last drive of the war. (Courtesy of Alice Inez Cummins and the Office of the Chaplain, 2nd Army, Baltimore, Maryland.)

This photograph shows the remains of victims at Buchenwald, a death camp of the Nazi regime. The remaining prisoners were liberated on April 11, 1945. (Courtesy of Margaret Wells Brooks; from the collection of Norris Eugene Wells. Robert Watkins helped with the distribution of the photograph.)

First Lt. Charles B. Hanna served as a doctor in the medical corps. He was able to attend the Nuremberg War Trials and concluded his duty after his station at Vienna, Austria. Dr. Hanna later established a medical practice in Spartanburg. (Courtesy of Dr. and Mrs. Charles B. Hanna.)

Cpl. Warren E. Baker, 3rd Armored Division, "Spearhead," served in the U.S. Army. He participated in the Ardennes, Rhineland, and Central Europe campaigns. Before his discharge on December 2, 1945, he earned the Bronze Star Medal, the EAME Campaign Medal with three Bronze Service Stars, the World War II Victory Medal, and the Good Conduct Medal. He had the honor of chauffeuring President Harry S Truman when Truman inspected the 3rd Armored Division and the 84th Infantry Division in Frankfurt, Germany. (Courtesy of Laree Baker George.)

M.Sgt. Ambrose Hudgens, Laundry Company, 680th Quartermaster Section Headquarters, 7th Army, received assignment to, among other places, Kaiserlautren, Germany. He earned the World War II Victory Medal, the German Occupation Medal, the Good Conduct Medal, and the Honorable Discharge Medal. This line drawing was a presentation by Sven, a comrade. (Courtesy of Ambrose Hudgens.)

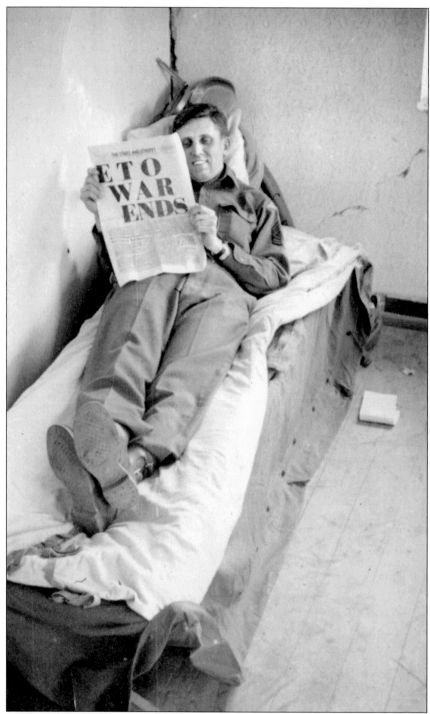

Ambrose Hudgens still remembers vividly the end of World War II in Europe. "On May 7, I heard the first V-E Day announcement at Ellwangen, Germany, which is about 20 miles south of Wurzberg." Resting on his cot, M.Sgt. Ambrose Hudgens reads from *The Stars and Stripes* about the end of the war in Europe. (Courtesy of Ambrose Hudgens.)

Nine

ENDING THE WAR (1945)
IWO JIMA, OKINAWA,
THE SURRENDER OF JAPAN

From the newly established air bases in the Marianas Islands, B-29 Superfortress bombers conducted numerous raids on the Japanese home islands. The purpose of these raids was to break the will of the Japanese people and their rulers. On February 19, 1945, the U.S. Marine Corps V Amphibious Corps began a 36-day campaign to secure the island of Iwo Jima. The resulting battle was the most famous one of World War II.

The photo above shows the 4th Marine Division coming ashore from landing crafts onto the black sands of Iwo Jima. (Courtesy of the U.S. Marines Corps.)

Taking part in these operations was Cpl. Ben J. De Luca, who was a proud rifleman ("mud marine") of the 3rd Battalion, 24th Regiment, 4th Marine Division. He came ashore in the third wave and was wounded so severely by mortar fire that, when he returned home in September, he had to be carried ashore on a stretcher. For his services in Iwo Jima, Saipan, and Tinian, De Luca received the Purple Heart, Silver Star Medal, Asiatic Pacific Campaign Medal with two Bronze Service Stars, American Defense Service Medal, American Campaign Medal, World War II Victory Medal, and U.S. Marine Corps Meritorious Service Medal. His unit received two Presidential Unit Citations and the Navy Unit Citation. (Courtesy of Ben J. De Luca.)

Cardinal Wilsey Wright Jr., who retired after 20 years from the U.S. Navy as a chief hospital corpsman, served in a Marine Corps unit on Iwo Jima for the duration of the entire campaign. Most of his service was in the Pacific. He also served at Virginia, Pearl Harbor, Charleston, the Canal Zone, Texas, and on board the USS *Warrington*. (Courtesy of Mrs. C.W. Wright Jr. and Dr. Randy Wright.)

For his services, Cardinal Wilsey Wright Jr. received the American Defense Service Medal, Asiatic-Pacific Campaign Medal, National Defense Service Medal, Good Conduct Medal (second, third, and fourth awards), World War II Victory Medal, and Navy Unit Citation. In his letter of commendation at Wright's retirement, his commanding officer recognized Wright for "continuously demonstrating an excellent character in the highest traditions of the U.S. Navy." (Courtesy of Mrs. C.W. Wright Jr. and Dr. Randy Wright.)

Sgt. Allen Clark Sr., 4th Marine Division, U.S. Marine Corps, participated in Saipan, Tinian, and Iwo Jima. He saved fellow Marine Gene Luckey's life on March 11, 1945, after a Japanese shell explosion buried Luckey. Luckey said he "awoke once and someone was pulling me to the beach. A flare lit up his profile and I could see him clearly. It has been over 50 years, and I can still see [the mere acquaintance who saved my life and whose first name I did not even know.]" A photo of the two in *Life/ Look* enabled Luckey to identify his savior, he told *Rockdale* (Texas) *Messenger* reporter Mike Brown in 1995, but only after Clark's death could Luckey make contact with the family. Clark, who was overseas for 20 months, was best known as Dorman High School principal for 11 years. (Courtesy of Ann Clark Webb and Allen O. Clark Jr.)

Cpl. Clyde Everett Rice, 2nd Battalion, 2nd Division, U.S. Marine Corps, participated in actions against the enemy on Saipan, Okinawa, Ryukyu Islands, and in the postwar occupation of Nagasaki, Japan. Upon his discharge, he received the Good Conduct Medal and the Honorable Discharge Medal. (Courtesy of Rachel Rice.)

J. Paul Rice, shown here, and his brothers Clyde and Frank all served in the Pacific in U.S. Marine Corps. (Courtesy of Rachel Rice.)

S.Sgt. Charles E. Collins, Battery C, 325th Anti-aircraft Artillery Searchlight Battalion, served during the occupation of Japan during 1945–1946. He was a mess sergeant and was a brother of Broadus Collins. He supervised eight men who ran a mess hall that fed 246 military personnel. Charles earned the Asiatic-Pacific Campaign Medal, the World War II Victory Medal, the Occupation of Japan Ribbon, and the Good Conduct Medal. After the war, he was best known as an employee of the Spartanburg District Seven school system. (Courtesy of Helen Collins.)

Cpt. Frank A. Lyles, 303rd Infantry Regiment, 97th Division, participated in the Rhineland Campaign; he remembers being "shot at and missed." He earned the Combat Infantryman's Badge, the Expert Infantryman's Badge, and the EAME Campaign Medal. He received a transfer to Japan and served in the Army of Occupation as an information and education officer. For his services, he received the Asiatic-Pacific Campaign Medal, the American Campaign Medal, the World War II Victory Medal, and the Japanese Occupation Medal. Frank and his brother Bill joined their father, Thomas Minter Lyles, in his law practice in Spartanburg after the war. (Courtesy of Frank A. Lyles.)

S.Sgt. Louis Rolen served as a rifleman in B Company, 128th RCT, 32nd Infantry Division of Luzon, P.I. He also served as manager of the NCO Club, Naka, Japan, 27th "Wolfhound" Regiment, 25th Infantry Division. He earned the Asiatic -Pacific Medal with Bronze Battle Star, Philippine Liberation Medal with one Bronze Service Star, Combat Infantryman's Badge, American Campaign Medal, World War II Victory Medal, and Good Conduct Medal. (Courtesy of Louis W. Rolen.)

Henry G. Flynn Jr. served in the U.S. Merchant Marine from July 1945 until August 1946. He enlisted in the U.S. Army in October 1946 and served in the occupation of Japan from January 1947 until January 1948. (Courtesy of Henry G. Flynn and family and Rev. Thomas C. Moore.)

Ten

DOING OUR PART (1941–1945)
SERVING ON THE HOMEFRONT

Over 16 million men and women served in the armed forces during World War II. Countless others labored on the homefront. The duties included working in defense industries, maintaining farms and households, raising money for "E" bonds, operating factories, providing entertainment for the soldiers, praying for the safe return of loved ones, and keeping the home fires burning. Important activities to elevate the troops' morale included sending packages to those away from home and maintains a steady flow of correspondence.

Billy Joe Byars (sixth child from the right) remembers well the "E" bond drives and this celebration at Drayton Mill. Billy Joe's beloved older brother Volney Lee Byars served during World War II. (Courtesy of Billy Joe Byars.)

Volney Lee Byars grew up in Spartanburg and is shown here in front of the house where he was born. He attended Whitney School for a short period of time but lived most of his life in the Drayton community. He graduated from Wofford College and was the pride of the family because he was the first to earn a college education. (Courtesy of Billy Joe Byars.)

Second Lt. Volney Lee Byars, Company A, 23rd Infantry, 2nd Infantry Division, "Indianhead," wrote to his wife and son from France. He told them of having a bath and clean clothes for the first time in 33 days. He said he would always love her and "would always be yours." Two days later, he was dead. Byars had come ashore on D-Day+1 and had been in France for 35 days when he was killed in action on July 12, 1944, near St. Lo, France. Byars was buried in Normandy Cemetery, St. Laurent-sur-Mer, France. He earned posthumously the Silver Star and the Purple Heart. (Courtesy of Billy Joe Byars.)

Second Lt. Charles D. Ashmore, U.S. Marine Corps, served in the Panama Canal Zone for 14 months. His unit was charged with preventing sabotage. In July 1944, he received assignment to the Marine Corps Institute in Washington, D.C.; the educational institution offered Marines correspondence courses that could lead to high-school diplomas. He retired as a captain in January 1946 and earned the American Campaign Medal. Dr. Ashmore came to Converse College in 1958 and served as dean of the College of Arts and Sciences until his 1982 retirement. (Courtesy of Charles D. Ashmore.)

Sgt. Charles Herbert Bonner was a military policeman with the U.S. Army. His station was the Panama Canal Zone, where he had the opportunity to learn Spanish. His next assignment was to Puerto Rico, where he taught English to Spanish-speaking soldiers. His special memory was an Easter Sunday at a sunrise service in Panama; a large, colorful bird landed near them and began to sing. The minister halted the service so that the men could listen to the serenade. Bonner was a graduate of Wofford College and retired from teaching at Sumter High School. (Courtesy of Alice B. Greene.)

Cpt. William C. Lyles of the U.S. Army served as a coastal artillery unit commander in Galapagos Island, Ecuador, for two years and one month. He served also as a harbor entrance control post officer at Fort Story, Virginia. He ended the war as an intelligence staff officer. He was a graduate of The Citadel and the University of South Carolina Law School. Bill and his brother Frank joined their father Thomas Minter Lyles in his law practice in Spartanburg after the war. (Courtesy of Bill Lyles.)

Pvt. 1st Class Ernest F. Washington, Headquarters and Headquarters Detachment, Section 1, SCU 1457, drove a two-and-a-half ton truck and performed all the associated duties of transporting men and materials. For his services, he received the American Theater Medal, the World War II Victory Medal, and the Good Conduct Medal. He was stationed for a while at Camp Croft and met his wife Alice Virginia Powell (Washington) at Smith's Drug Store in Spartanburg. He was an employee of Jenkins School in 1953. (Courtesy of Joyce Washington.)

Sgt. Edward Sellars served in the U.S. Army Air Forces at Spence Field, Moultrie, Georgia, and at Craig Field in Selma, Alabama. He was a crew chief of 12 men who refueled the aircraft. He earned the American Theater Service Medal and the Good Conduct Medal. He signed this photo, "Just me!" (Courtesy of Helen Collins and family.)

Seaman 1st Class Robert D. Putman served on the USS *Randolph*. His ship patrolled the Mediterranean and the North Atlantic. He earned the American Campaign Medal, the World War II Victory Medal, and the Good Conduct Medal. (Courtesy of Robert D. Putman and Rev. Thomas C. Moore.)

WO (jg) John Earl Bakke served in the U.S. Army as a personnel officer at Camp Croft, Spartanburg, South Carolina. He also served in Texas and Florida. His occupation before military service was with the Studebaker-Aviation Corporation. Here John Earle Bakke is pictured with his wife, Eva Lou Turpin Bakke, just after their wedding ceremony in Gramling. John Earle Bakke met Eva Lou Turpin while he was stationed at Camp Croft. Bakke moved from Chicago to South Carolina after the war. (Courtesy of Karen and Martha Bakke.)

James Fred Casey Jr. served in the Engineers of the U.S. Army. His duty stations included Fort Belvoir, Virginia. Casey married Aleth McCurry (a sister of Forrest, Raymond, and Neubert McCurry) and was drafted in 1942. He was released from duty after the birth of their child Elaine. Casey received a second draft notice in 1944 and entered service again. It was indeed an unusual occurrence to be drafted twice. (Courtesy of Mrs. James Fred Casey Jr.)

Sgt. Forrest T. McCurry served in the U.S. Army Air Forces in Texas. Forrest loved animals and is pictured astride a horse on the family farm. His family included sister Aleth McCurry Casey, brother-in-law James Fred Casey Jr., and brothers Raymond and Neubert McCurry. (Courtesy of Mrs. James Fred Casey Jr.)

Lizzie Dillard, a twin, married Harold Hayes, also a twin. During the war, Lizzie worked at Silver's Dime Store in Spartanburg. She recalls writing regularly to Harold. On one occasion, her employer saw her writing a letter; when he asked her what she was doing, she answered honestly, and he never mentioned the incident again. Harold remembered carrying a lock of her auburn hair in his wallet throughout the war. When the interviewer asked about obtaining a photo of Lizzie for the volume, Harold immediately produced from his wallet this photo from 1945. (Courtesy of Lizzie and Harold Hayes.)

Cpl. Mary E. Mason served in the Women's Army Auxiliary Corps (WAAC). She served with the 323 Headquarters Squadron, AB Squadron W, at Muroc Army Air Field in Muroc, California. As indicated by this large class, many women felt compelled to help their country. (Courtesy of Rev. Thomas C. Moore.)

Virginia "Gin" Owens (Dean) from Drayton, South Carolina, entered the WAACs in April 1943. She earned the title of "the Typical American Woman Soldier" and received national publicity. After being stationed in New Jersey, she was sent to the Miami Army Air Field. It was here that she met Wallace G. Dean. (Courtesy of Mrs. Wally Dean.)

S.Sgt. Wallace "Wally" G. Dean was stationed at Miami Army Air Field and met his future wife, Virginia "Gin" Owens Dean, there. In 1945, he married the woman the local paper had headlined "Spartanburg Girl as Typical American Woman Soldier." Spartanburg remembers Wally Dean best as a successful basketball coach and assistant principal at Spartanburg High School. (Courtesy of Mrs. Wally Dean.)

Jane Klim (Hughes) was a registered nurse at Old Mercy Hospital, Springfield, Massachusetts, from 1942 until 1945. On a trip to Spartanburg to assist her brother Henry Klim and his wife after the birth of their child, she met John P. Hughes. They married and are still married today. Most people in Spartanburg know the couple best through their family business, Pic-A-Book at Hillcrest Shopping Center; the store has been in operation since 1971. (Courtesy of Jane Klim Hughes.)

Bess Rice Ball, a graduate of the Converse College School of Music, toured with the USO group "the Concert Hour." Bessie is quick to say that it "was a high class" hour of quality music with "nothing coarse." The group sailed from Los Angeles to Manila in January 1946. From the Philippines, they traveled to several places in Japan, including Tokyo and Yokohama. She was in Nagasaki about one year after the bombing and remembers the devastation and how frightened the children were. When she returned to the United States, she met William L. Ball Jr., the new preacher in her home church. They were married for more than 50 years. (Courtesy of Bessie Rice Ball.)

Mary Wilson Tucker Arrowood worked in the defense industry—specifically the Charlotte Shell Plant. Mary's job was helping to prepare the powder for insertion in the 40 mm shells. Mary remembers how her hands would often become red, sore, and rough from handling the cordite. After her marriage to Dan Ray Arrowood, she moved to his parents' home and changed employment. (Courtesy of Mary Wilson Tucker Arrowood.)

Imogene (Jean) Davis (Corne) spent the summer of her junior year in high school with her brother and his wife at Fort Meade, Maryland. She worked as "a soda jerk" at the drug store in the Post Exchange. After graduation, she returned to Fort Meade as a worker in the Postal Directory, where she rerouted letters to the service personnel. Here she met (and later married) Charles William Corne. This collage shows them in a 1937 Ford. After their marriage, they eventually located in South Carolina. (Courtesy of Imogene Davis Corne.)

Spartanburg was the site of several secret meetings to discuss the possible use and effects of the atomic bomb in World War II. James F. Byrnes had just retired as Director of War, Mobilization, and Reconstruction and had returned to town on April 8, 1945. At the Crystal Drive home of Donald Russell, the Interim Committee, composed of political leaders, scientists, and diplomats, met several times to weigh opinions for and against employing the device. The home in Converse Heights is now owned by Fred Moffitt. The private residence is visible from the public road. (Courtesy of James M. Walker.)

Converse College students were aware of the scarcity of farm workers and the necessity of harvesting the crops quickly. College buses transported students to the cotton fields of the area. Pictured are students picking cotton alongside college administrators and others aiding the war effort. (Courtesy of Converse College and Dr. James G. Harrison, Mickel Archives.)

With the outbreak of war in Europe, President Roosevelt and Army Chief of Staff Gen. George C. Marshall began the massive preparation of what would be 16 million service personnel. Myriad training facilities sprang up across the country. On December 12, 1940, the federal government began moving more than 200 landowners and their families from an 18,000-acre plot in Spartanburg to 635 prefabricated units in Pacolet. One of these landowners was the father of Harold Hayes. The Farm Security Administration and the Office of War Information documented some of these families and the new facilities; Jack Delano made this photo. (Library of Congress, Prints and Photographs Division, FSA-OWI Collection, LC-USF34-043604-D DLC.)

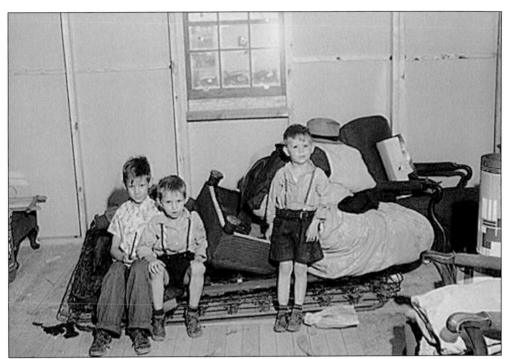

This photograph by Jack Delano illustrates the dislocation that occurred with the uprooting of families for the establishment of Camp Croft. (Library of Congress, Prints and Photographs Division, FSA-OWI Collection, LC-USF34-043825-D DLC.)

Main Entrance Gate, Camp Croft

The camp in Spartanburg bore the name of Camp Croft, named for Maj. Gen. Edward Croft of the U.S. Army. Croft was the son of Civil War officer Col. Edward Croft, The Citadel Class of 1856; he served in 14th SC Regiment, McGowan's Brigade, and suffered wounds at Gettysburg. This postcard shows the front gates of Camp Croft. (Courtesy of U.S. Army Signal Corps.)

The Camp Croft facilities included a bakery to supply up to 25,000 men, a laundry to serve up to 20,000 men, a 720-bed hospital, a radio station and post office to aid communication, a telephone exchange with 250 lines, an enlisted men's club with "one of the best dance floors in the Piedmont," three theaters, classrooms, and training facilities. One of the barracks housed John Earl Bakke, the future husband of Eva Lou Turpin Bakke. The arrow indicates Bakke's upstairs quarters. (Courtesy of Karen and Martha Bakke.)

Between 65,000 and 75,000 troops moved through the Camp Croft U.S. Army Infantry Replacement Training Center each year. Basic training usually consisted of six weeks of rigorous activities. Most infantrymen mastered march-and-drill exercises before their training. Route marching, pitching tents, weapons familiarization, morale-building classes, personal hygiene, small unit tactics, physical fitness exercises, and military law and customs formed part of the curriculum of each recruit. (Courtesy of U.S. Army.)

Spartanburg City had a population of 32,249 in 1940. The 1940 county population was 127,733. Three higher education facilities in the area were Converse College, Wofford College, and (now) Spartanburg Methodist College. At the time, 11 public schools and 41 textile plants existed. Four railroads served the city. The Spartanburg Chamber of Commerce described Camp Croft in 1940 as "One of the beautiful camps of the army in the South." One of the favorite centers for rest and relaxation was Main Street in Spartanburg with its Smith Drug Store, where Ernest Washington met his wife-to-be, Alice Virginia Powell Washington. (Courtesy of Spartanburg Chamber of Commerce.)

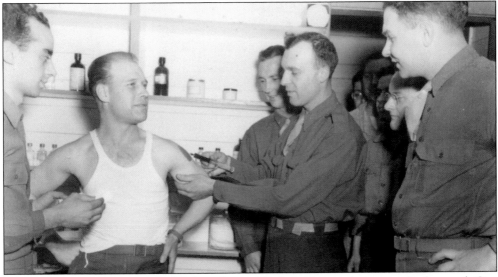

Camp Croft was a melting pot that brought together young men from every background. One of the soldiers there was a naturalized citizen of 1943, Henry Kissinger from Germany, who received his training at Camp Croft. Another young man who cycled through Camp Croft was Edward "Ed" Koch, a mayor of New York City. Mel Allen, longtime radio voice of the New York Yankees, also trained at Camp Croft. Another trainee was future U.S. Senator Alan Cranston. All of these men—and countless others—received training at Camp Croft after immunizations. (Courtesy of Roger Wesley Goodwin and Meg Goodwin Cooksey.)

Kitchen Patrol was one of the first duties any recruit had to perform. The most famous chore was that of peeling enough potatoes for the entire unit. After rising early in the morning for roll call, calisthenics, and chow, a day spent scouring the pots and pans or peeling the potatoes would exhaust any recruit. (Courtesy of Roger Wesley Goodwin and Meg Goodwin Cooksey.)

Recruits had to become familiar with a variety of weapons. These might include the Garand rifle (M-1), the Thompson submachine gun ("Tommy" gun), and the .45-caliber pistol. (Courtesy of Roger Wesley Goodwin and Meg Goodwin Cooksey.)

The American soldier, most familiar with the workings of the internal combustion engine of all combatants in World War II, could improvise and repair equipment in order to push forward. This skill and knowledge had come from his earliest childhood experiences: working in the fields, working at the service station, and "fixing up" the family vehicle. American service personnel would acquire their more formal training in the motor pool. (Courtesy of Roger Wesley Goodwin and Meg Goodwin Cooksey.)

The American Army was willing to learn from the enemy. With the success of the German "Blitzkreig" in Europe, the Americans rapidly established armored divisions. This photograph shows an M-1 Stuart tank at speed on a typical training ground. American armored divisions would be equipped both with speedy tanks like these and with the larger and heavier M-4 Shermans. (Courtesy of Roger Wesley Goodwin and Meg Goodwin Cooksey.)

Essential to any training group and in the battles to follow was the medic with his knowledge of first aid. (Courtesy of Roger Wesley Goodwin and Meg Goodwin Cooksey.)

All soldiers carried a small first-aid pack and a sewing kit ("army housewife"). Depending on the denomination of the enlisted, the pocket might also contain scriptures and even a rosary. This metal clad Testament, was in the possession of Anita Price Davis's father, Arthur Fred Price, when he stepped on a landmine on December 28, 1944, shows the results of the explosion. (Courtesy of Anita Price Davis.)

During duty-free time, service personnel could enjoy sports, letter writing, listening to the radio, playing cards, or shooting craps. (Courtesy of Roger Wesley Goodwin and Meg Goodwin Cooksey.)

To ensure a variety of reading for the enlisted even in the most remote places of the world, the Council on Books in Wartime developed a new type of book designed to fit the pocket of the fatigues. These paperback volumes were about 5.5 inches by 4 inches. Both classics and current books in an unabridged format were available free of charge in an overseas edition for the Armed Forces. The Special Services Division, A.S.F., for the army, and the Bureau of Naval Personnel for the navy distributed these books. The Editions for the Armed Services, Inc., a non-profit organization established by the Council on Books in Wartime, provided the publishing. (Courtesy of Anita Price Davis.)

Joseph George "Joe" Nohra remembers the mobile Post Exchange at Camp Croft with its "sandwiches, hot dogs, hamburgers, cakes, pies, and do-nuts" delivered right to your door! (Courtesy of Joe Nohra.)

Railways and troop convoys transported equipment and American personnel across the country. Convoys were a frequent sight on highways of the nation. Anita Price Davis still recalls the excitement she would feel each time a troop convoy passed her home. As a small child, she hurried to the front yard to wave and yell in hopes her father—or, after the death of her father, her uncles—might be on the truck, see her, and return her wave. (Courtesy of Roger Wesley Goodwin and Meg Goodwin Cooksey.)

Entire divisions would embark on great liners like the *Queen Mary*, the *Aquatania*, and other Cunard liners. Harold Hayes, who married Lizzie Dillard Hayes, remembers his journey on the *Queen Mary*. (Courtesy of Harold Hayes.)

To remember the service personnel, Drayton Baptist Church displayed a banner with blue stars for each person in service. If bad news came, the grieving families and friends changed the blue star to gold. Volney Lee Byars, a member of the Drayton Baptist Church, lost his life and is represented by a gold star. (Courtesy of Billy Joe Byars.)

Spartan Mills in Spartanburg County proudly boasted a roster of "Spartan Mills Employees in Our Country's Service." One of the names listed is that of Volney Lee Byars, Billy Joe Byars's older brother. (Courtesy of Billy Joe Byars.)

Uncle Sam, a constant image across the nation, reminded everyone of the need for sacrifice, devotion, and service. The federal government published this poster. (Courtesy of Anita Price Davis.)

Duncan Park hosts this memorial to the ones from Spartanburg County who died in the service of their nation. Veterans constructed and donated the archway "in memory of our fallen comrades who fought and died" to help secure freedom for us all. The walls behind the archway contain the names of those who died in World Wars I and II; it lists also the Korean, Vietnam, Persian Gulf, Afghanistan, and Iraq Wars. The memorial was and remains a project of the DAV, the VFW, the FFA of Dorman High, the American Legion, and veterans across the county. (Courtesy of James M. Walker.)

The town of Cowpens is the home of another memorial to county veterans—both living and dead. The memorial is dedicated "To the memory of those who made the supreme sacrifice and in honor of all who served their country in time of need." A committee of 10 veterans worked with Wilhelmina Dearybury on the project starting in 2002. (Courtesy of James M. Walker.)

Prayers and Wishes
Troy O. Edwards

When leaving our homes, loved ones and friends,
Our big task in the army seems so hard to begin.
Better to have your prayers than your wishes.

As we journey down the road in tremble and fear,
It seems we are leaving everything
Precious and dear.
Better to have your prayers than your wishes.

When arriving in camp somewhat lonely and sad,
We look around and wonder: has the world gone mad?
Better to have your prayers than your wishes.

Into this changed life, which is
everything but happy and gay,
We begin to wonder, think, and pray.
Better to have your prayers than your wishes.

In the hurry and rush at the
beginning of this war thing,
We look up to God in spirit and sing.
Better to have your prayers than your wishes.

As we think of the challenges to face
With all our might,
Something seems to tell us boys we are
"In the right."

At last when we get in the thick of the fight,
It is an ugly, dirty, and bloody sight.
It's better to have your prayers than your wishes.

Pvt. 1st Class Troy Oma Edwards, 814th Tank Destroyer Battalion saw combat during the time of the Battle of the Bulge. (Courtesy of Troy O. Edwards.)

Staff Sergeant Eugene C. Tabbot, 3rd Combat Cargo Squadron, United States Army Air Forces. participated in the China Burma India Theater of Operations. Tabbot's unit transported supplies to Allied Forces in Burma and supported offensives against Mandalay and Rangoon. The unit transported over 50,000 drums of fuel and carried over 5,000 mules to China; Tabbot remembers the holes in the plane from the hooves of the agitated animals. Tabbot recalls dropping paratroopers and evacuating the wounded. For his services he earned the Distinguished Flying Cross, the Air Medal with three oak leaf clusters, the Good Conduct Medal, the American Campaign Medal, the Asiatic Pacific Campaign Medal with one Bronze Service Star, the World War II Victory Medal, and the Honorable Discharge Pin. (Courtesy of Eugene C. Tabbot.)

INDEX